# The Pocket Guide to Beer

featuring the **BeerTubeMap**™

Joe Dick and
Nikki Welch

BIRLINN

First published in 2018 by
Birlinn Limited
West Newington House
10 Newington Road
Edinburgh
EH9 1QS

*www.birlinn.co.uk*

ISBN 978 1 78027 489 8

British Library Cataloguing-in-Publication Data
A catalogue record for this book is available
from the British Library

Designed and typeset by Mark Blackadder
BeerTubeMap artwork by Go! Bang! Creative Ltd

Printed and bound by PNB Print Ltd, Latvia

# Contents

# Introduction

The beer world has undergone a revolution over the past twenty years, and is now more exciting than ever. The flourishing craft brewery scene is showing no sign of slowing down, which brings a fresh take on beer styles old and new, and wine shops and bars have longer and longer lists of beers available.

All this is excellent news for beer drinkers and non-beer drinkers alike. The opportunity to expand your drinking repertoire or find a beer you actually like is far greater now than ever before, whatever your preferences. But it isn't always easy to navigate these styles and work out where to start or which direction to head in. Beer labels are pretty amazing to look at, but don't always help point you to what they mean, and listed on a blackboard many of the names look so daunting they are often ignored.

When Joe and I embarked on this journey I already understood the principles of beer, and had an idea of what I liked, but what I couldn't imagine was how much my beer drinking would change through the creation of the BeerTubeMap. Joe brought a deep understanding of beer styles and brewing to the process from the industry side. By tasting all the beers side by side, we discovered flavour connections beyond the accepted wisdom of the beer world and surprised ourselves with some of the flavour patterns.

Beer is naturally quite a geeky subject, and at each station of the map we've attempted to distil the technical reasons why each beer tastes the way it does, with some useful chat about the style. To avoid getting too technical we have created a glossary of all the geeky beer terms at the back so you can impress your friends with your beerspeak!

We hope this book and the BeerTubeMap will help you to expand your tastes as much as it did ours.

Cheers!

Nikki and Joe

## How to use the BeerTubeMap

It is unlikely you will read this book cover to cover. Instead, use the different sections to explore the beers on the BeerTubeMap, improve your beer tasting and get hints and tips on practical things like buying beer and food matching. Dip in and out as the mood takes you.

The beginning of the book contains some practical information on how the BeerTubeMap works and how to use it, as well as a guide to beer tasting and beer flavours. You might want to read it first to get the most out of the book.

The main section is dedicated to the BeerTubeMap and flavours on it. Read up on your favourite beers, or if you spot a station that's close to your favourite find out more to get a sense of whether it's for you – knowing that there is no substitute for tasting the real thing. To help understand your tastes better, look up a beer when you are drinking it to get a sense of where the flavours are coming from. The stations are organised by line, and the line colours are on the page edges to help you navigate between them easily.

The final section contains 'how to' guides, including buying and sourcing beer and food matching, so take a look when you're after a bit of beer inspiration. There's also a handy section on what to do if you get a beer that tastes wrong, which we've called 'Troubleshooting'.

The BeerTubeMap is a flavour map of beer, organising styles and types of beer from around the world, traditional and new, by taste and texture rather than by geography or brewing method.

This means you can explore a wide range of beer styles just by knowing what you (or someone else) like or dislike. It is designed for everyone, whether you are a self-classified geek or completely new to beer, to inspire and assist you in your beer exploration.

The key to using this map and guide is that you explore your own tastes and preferences. Taste is a completely subjective experience and anyone who tells you what you should (or should not) like is doing you a disservice. All the beers in this book and on the BeerTubeMap have their merits; it is down to you to decide whether that beer is for you.

**How it works:**

O  Each line has its own flavour profile, and as you travel along the line this evolves. For some lines the flavour theme is quite narrow, for others there is a greater evolution, crossing styles. On all lines the flavours run from light to intense.

O  Each station represents a different type of beer and these are divided into the following categories: regional speciality; production method; style; or a style that brewers put their own twist on. There is a chapter with more information on each station and recommendations for specific beers available in pubs, bars or shops that are good examples if you want to find one. There is more information on how the stations are divided in the icons section (p. 10).

O  The intersections on the BeerTubeMap represent beers that have become classics or are cross-sections of flavour from which you could travel in a number of different directions.

**Public service announcement**

It is impossible to cover every beer or brewing style out there, so this is a representation of the beer world as we see it. Brewing is a creative process and each brewer will make their own version of a style of beer based on their location, ingredients, climate and preferences. The stations and descriptions refer to a classic interpretation or benchmark of each style (unless specified).

### Using the map

If you already know what you like:

O Find your favourite station on the map. Each station represents a style of beer: you'll generally find it named somewhere on the beer label although it may not be the most prominent wording, e.g. American IPA, Blonde or Weissbier.

O If you have a favourite beer brand check the beer index at the back of the book to see if it's there – it will send you to the correct station on the map.

O Try the stations to either side of your favourite; these will be most similar.

O Continue along the line in that direction trying the next beer. Be aware that you may reach a point that is your limit for that line. If that's the case go to the nearest intersection and try a new line.

If you are feeling adventurous:

O Find a beer you are familiar with.

O Head to the other end of the line that it is on, for a different take on the same flavour profile.

O Or try a completely different line and pick a different beer from there. It might be worth doing this in a pub or bar where they offer you tasters!

If you are new to beer:

O Head to **Starting points**, p. 13.

If you are buying a gift:

O Find out your recipient's favourite beer.

○ Select a different, more uncommon, beer from the surrounding stations.

For more suggestions head to the **Having Fun with Beer at Home** section (p. 128), but most importantly, get tasting!

## Icons

To help you navigate the BeerTubeMap every station has an icon to denote what category of beer it represents. Most beer styles differ due to the way that they are produced and so are grouped under the 'Production method' icon. However, some are produced in specified geographical areas under stricter conditions and are considered 'Regional specialities'; they tend to be very similar whichever brewery they come from. On the other hand, some other styles mean a brewer can be more creative in their production to add their 'Twist', and these can vary more in flavour from one brewer to another. Because of these differences, individual beers produced under each station may differ a little or a lot, and the icon should help point to which is which.

###  PRODUCTION METHOD

Production method is the most common type of station on the BeerTubeMap. The beers with this icon have all been produced using a similar 'recipe' of ingredients, grain, yeast, hops, fermentation and ageing, which means they will share flavours and texture. So, for example, a Weissbier will always use a Weissbier yeast and wheat as the grain to ensure the distinctive bubblegum flavour and frothy head. Although each brewer's interpretation will differ these beers are not 'Regional specialities' (see p. 11) so can be made anywhere in the world, sometimes with local ingredients which will affect the flavour. The station page will highlight any major differences between beers produced in different countries, or variations that you might find within that specific production method.

**Public service announcement**
In some cases one brand, or producer, has become synonymous with the style; if this is the case both the production method and the brand (producer) are listed.

 **REGIONAL SPECIALITIES**

Some beers are so rooted in the tradition of where they are made, and why they are made there, that they aren't replicated by other brewers around the world. This means that they have a very defined style, flavour and texture and it is unlikely to vary much between producers. These beers speak of tradition and heritage, and have often been made in the same way for centuries. This tradition extends to the way they are served, which often includes a specific shape of glass and a traditional food accompaniment. Whilst the production doesn't necessarily travel, the beers do and some of these names are seen on bars and shops in every corner of the world.

 **STYLE**

Whilst most beers are easily categorised by their production method or region of origin, some of our stations are less established styles; the beers within them share a family but the flavours might have been reached by a less defined process. Take, for example, Coffee Stout: it isn't yet an industry-wide style which has a defined recipe, instead brewers are making their own versions, in their own way. They carry the 'Style' icon as a recognised style of beer and you'll find any beer with that name will have similar flavours and texture. In the main, the station name appears on the label.

**TWIST**

One of the exciting things about the current new wave of brewing is the creativity and influence a brewer can have over their output: brewers cannot stop themselves playing with the recipe, ingredients or method to create something unique. Which means, in a way, that all beers are open to interpretation. All very exciting! However, some production methods or styles are more open than others. The 'Twist' icon means that the beers within this station often have a twist on the central style or production method. This is mostly done by adding an ingredient, known in the beer world as an adjunct, like the addition of grapefruit to Gose or IPA.

## Starting points

It's all well and good if you know what you like when it comes to beer. Or even if you've tried a few and have got a bit of an idea of what you've enjoyed, or have not enjoyed, for that matter. But what happens if you just don't know where to start – or if you have not yet had a good experience? Not even a BeerTubeMap can help you out if you don't have a starting point ... Which is why we've created three starting points on the map, identified by this icon ➹ to help you work out which area to explore.

Ideally, try the three beers consecutively and pick out the one whose flavours you prefer, then explore the stations closest to it. It may not be love at first sip; if it isn't, pick the most palatable one and then explore beers that are a couple of stations away.

### Kölsch (see p. 27 for more information)
Kölsch sits at the meeting point of lager and ale, so it's a great starting point if you want more than a lager but not quite an ale. Lagers have got a bit of a reputation for bland, fizzy pints in sports bars, but there's a whole world of difference out there, so try this and you might change your mind. Kölsch has been around in Germany for a long time but it has recently become a regular feature in bars and shops around the UK so you'll find it relatively easily.

**Start here ...**

... if you want something light and refreshing.

**Where next?**

- O After more of the same? Travel the Lager Line and try Helles and Kellerbier for more refreshing but tasty light beers.
- O Want something a bit punchier? Head south on the Aromatic Line towards Pale Ales and IPAs.
- O Want something a bit more robust? Change onto the Central Line for the maltier ales and bitters.

**American IPA (see p. 45 for more information)**

It would be hard not to include American IPA as a starting point, partly because it is almost impossible to avoid! It is not a shy beer, and has a dominant, bitter hop character that ranges from green and herbaceous to grapefruit peel and a refreshing bitterness. Quality can be variable and there are a lot of one-dimensional, commercial versions out there so it's worth looking at the 'Beers to look out for' section on the American IPA station to see the recommended breweries.

**Start here ...**

... if you like it pithy, and don't want to trawl the shops and bars to find your beer.

**Where next?**

- O Want something a bit lighter? Head north towards the less hoppy pale ales and lagers.
- O Love that aromatic hit? Head south towards the Belgian and wheat beers or east towards Double IPA for more hop action.
- O Want something with more oomph? Head west on the Discovery Line towards Amber Ale and Red Ale.

### Porter (see p. 94 for more information)

Porter is a big jump from the other two starting point beers, so it may feel like a step too far – don't let that put you off though. Porter is a rich, robust beer with layers of chocolate and coffee flavours. It isn't one to drink all night, but its full body and dark flavours can be very moreish and a nice change if you're not a fan of lighter beer styles.

### Start here ...

... if you want a more intense glass of beer.

### Where next?

O Find Porter a bit too much? Head east on the Central Line, there are a number of beers that share the dark, savoury flavours of Porter but are lighter in texture.

O Want something sweeter? If you've got a sweet tooth take the one-way loop at the bottom of the Indulgence Line and try the Milk Stout and Coffee Stout, both of which have a touch of the 'gourmand' about them. Or head west for the sweeter but powerful Scotch Ale and Barley Wine.

O Want something more intense? Head south to Imperial Stout for even more roasted coffee intensity.

### Public service announcement

Pronunciation is not specified in the main for these stations as you mostly say what you see. Many of them have Germanic origin and contain vowels wearing umlauts; it is worth noting that these have a slightly squashed sound, for example, the 'ö' in Kölsch is more like an 'uh' than an 'oh' sound, and the 'ä' in Märzen is closer to an 'eh' than an 'ah' sound. Most Ws are pronounced like a 'v', and 'ei' is pronounced like 'eye', so for example Weissbier sounds like 'vice-beer'. Any 'ch' sounds are soft, as in the Scottish word 'loch'. However, you don't need to adopt a foreign accent, people will understand you!

# Making the most of beer

As the beer world continues to expand and the choice increases, it is easy to become a bit overwhelmed and end up shopping within the confines of one style or one brand. The BeerTubeMap is designed to help open up the options, without too much geeky beer chat. Whether you're after a beer to impress over dinner, something to sip on the sofa or give as a gift, there are plenty of options out there, all you need to know is what your starting point on the map is.

The BeerTubeMap encourages you to take a step back from the cult of novelty that has taken over the beer world and explore your flavour preferences, as well as why you might switch your beer depending on the occasion, the time of day or night and what you're eating. Despite its humble roots there is quite a lot of beer snobbery and one-upmanship out there, especially when it comes to the 'newest' edition or brewery on the block. Ticking off all of the Double IPAs from a cult brewery is all well and good, but do you actually like what you're drinking?

You don't need to take it too seriously either, just take a moment to think about what you do (and don't) like about the beer you're drinking so you can start to make some more deliberate moves. If you're keen to develop your tastes it helps to sample two or more beers side by side; this helps you pick out the differences between them and gives you some contrast. Take your time to pick out the aromas, flavours and textures you like; to begin with all beer tastes like 'beer', but you'll soon start to find more depth and flavour.

## Modern brewing and artistic licence

Without the severe restrictions on production methods that the whisky and wine industries face, creativity and experimentation run wild in the beer world. Although this book is based on styles, new beers are constantly being produced which don't sit comfortably within any pre-existing style guidelines, and some can eventually break away to become entire style categories of their own. The rules are totally fluid, and nothing is off-limits.

The openness of brewers on social media, and the global economy, have allowed for information sharing and collaboration on an unprecedented scale. Breweries from tiny villages in sleepy Middle England are being invited to work with some of the biggest names in the beer world and the result is more creativity, innovation, shared knowledge and an increase in quality across the board.

The modern beer market is increasingly becoming consumer-led, and these consumers appear to have a never-ending thirst for new beers. This means brewers will continue to innovate and tweak even their core range of beers so, even if you continue to drink within just one station, you'll always find something new to consider.

## What influences flavour

The beer-making process is relatively simple, it mostly requires just four ingredients, yet the end product can differ enormously. Each ingredient or process can be manipulated to change the flavour or texture of a beer. At each station there are explanations of how that type of beer gets its specific flavours, but it helps to understand the basics behind these flavour influencers. Once you start discovering your favourite beers you can see which flavour influencers they have in common.

## Malt

The malt is the product of malting and roasting barley, and is the main ingredient in most beers. The way the barley is malted has a major influence on the end-flavour of beer as well as giving it its colour. Malting is the process of germinating and then applying heat to the barley grains to stop their progress, and it is this heat that has the most flavour impact. The kilns use a high heat to dry the barley, in essence roasting it. The longer and hotter it is roasted for, the darker and stronger the beer will be. A lightly roasted malt will produce a pale lager or ale where you don't really notice the malt taste. A golden roast will result in a more golden beer with a sweeter, more biscuity or bready character, whereas a darker roast will create more intense coffee and chocolate flavours. These darker roasts also tend to create more texture in the beer, giving them a fuller body. The resultant malt may have a speciality name, like Vienna Malt, due to the roasting level and qualities that this brings. The brewer's art is to blend together a selection of malts, known as a malt bill or grist, to create the exact flavour and textures they require for their beers.

## Yeast

Without fermentation, there would be no beer. Traditionally yeast was considered a magical, invisible ingredient; now it's a highly scientific tool used by brewers. In some beers the use of yeast is purely for the creation of alcohol: the yeast eats sugar and releases alcohol and carbon dioxide as by-products. But in other beers the yeast has other outputs which add complexity and flavour. There are two principal types of yeast used in beer: lager yeast and ale yeast. Lager yeasts are light and give off less flavour, they work at a long, low temperature, whereas ale yeasts are quick and flourish in a warm temperature: it is this warmth and speed which result in the fruity, spicy flavours in ales.

## Hops

The buzzword in craft beer is 'hoppy', referring to the bitter, zesty character that hops bring to beer, traditionally to balance

the sweetness of the malt and as a preservative or antioxidant. The term doesn't really tell the whole story as the type and origin of the hop make a big difference to the end flavour, as does the point at which they are added to the brewing process. Hops are the flowers of a climbing plant, *Humulus lupulus*, which grows across the northern hemisphere. The strains used in beer are split predominantly into European, British and US varieties, all of which have different flavour properties. These strains are all named, and modern brewers will sometimes name them on the label: Mosaic, Citra, Cascade etc.

Some hops are used to add bitterness and are introduced early in the boiling process to extract as much of the bitter character as possible; this bitterness can be measured using the International Bitterness Units scale (the IBU level). In contrast, aromatic hops are added at the latest stage of the boil so as not to quash their delicate aromatics. This commonly shows up as a slightly bitter citrus or grassy flavour, but it can also be floral, herby, resinous or tropical. The craze to make and drink extremely hoppy beers has led to the creation of a number of technological advances, most notably in the process of 'dry hopping', where more hops are added after the boiling process has finished to infuse even more of the aromatic hop flavours.

### Grain

Whilst malted barley is the key ingredient in beer, other grains can be used and this will impact on the end beer in terms of flavour, aroma, colour, texture and residual sweetness. Wheat is probably the most commonly used alternative grain, but unmalted barley, oats and rye are also added in differing quantities. These other grains contain different proteins and compounds, which during fermentation will change the resulting beer's flavour and texture, so the ratio of grains added to malted barley dictates how strong their influence is. For example, and very generally, wheat tends to add a bready character, oats a creamy texture and rye adds a spiciness.

## How beer is made

At its most basic, the beer-making process is pretty simple, however the brewer is making decisions at every step of the way that will affect the ultimate flavour, body and style of beer. Here we give a simplified view of the process to help you understand the differences as you read about each station.

○ **Germination** – Barley is harvested and sent to a maltster, who germinates the grains. The process of grain-sprouting releases starches and enzymes that are key to the fermentation process. The enzymes break down the starches into smaller sugars; without this the sugars are too large for the yeast to metabolise into alcohol. The level of enzymes the malt contains is known as its diastatic power, and this indicates the potential for the grain to convert starch to sugar. High levels mean the brewer can more efficiently convert the sugar, which in turn becomes alcohol, lower levels mean more starch is left, which can add texture and flavour to a beer, but less potential alcohol.

○ **Malting** – The germinated grains are then dried in a kiln to stop them growing any further and using up their sugars. This is where much of the toasted flavour and colour in beer comes from. The more intense the roast, the darker and toastier the flavours.

○ **Mash** – The malt is then crushed and mixed with hot water in the mash tun, essentially making a giant bowl of porridge. This allows enzymes contained within the malt to break down the starch granules into an array of fermentable sugars. The sugary, malty liquid produced is known as sweet wort. Different factors of the mashing process influence the make-up of the sugars and thus the fermentability of the wort, such as temperature, pH, water (known as 'liquor' in the brewing process) and time. It is the skill of the brewer to manipulate these factors to produce the type of wort he wishes to make. The sweet wort produced from mashing is able to provide all the nutrients required by yeast. The wort sits at an optimum temperature for sugar extraction and is then pumped from bottom to top to allow the mash to filter the wort and clarify it.

O **Run-off** – When ready the 'first runnings' are drawn off into the kettle, water is sprayed onto the grain to rinse the last of the sugars from it, and the rest of the wort is transferred to the kettle.

O **The boil** – The wort is then boiled, typically for an hour to ninety minutes, and hops are added. Hops added near the beginning of the boil add bitterness, hops added later in the boil contribute more aromatics. This boiling also sanitises the wort and further concentrates the sugar proportion in it.

O **Fermentation** – The wort is then cooled and transferred to a fermenter, where yeast is added and fermentation takes place. The sugars broken down during the mash phase are consumed by the yeast and converted into energy – the process of fermentation – and alcohol and carbon dioxide (the bubbles) are by-products of this process. Not all sugars can be used by the yeast and those that remain give the beer body. The yeast type and the temperature and length of fermentation all influence the final beer.

O **Conditioning and maturation** – Once fermentation is finished, the beer is not quite ready to leave the brewery – it is known as 'green beer' at this stage. It must undergo a period of maturation, or conditioning, so the yeast can remove the unpleasant flavour compounds produced during fermentation; this normally takes one to two weeks, traditionally even longer for lagers. The length and temperature of maturation depends on the type of beer being made, but generally beers are held at a temperature a few degrees lower than for fermentation so the yeast can 'clean up' the beer. The brewer can then cool the temperature further to help any large particles, mainly formed of yeast and hop matter, to drop out of suspension and stabilise the beer ready for packaging. It is at this stage that the carbon dioxide level (the fizz!) can be adjusted to suit the style of the beer.

O **Adjuncts** – These are other ingredients ranging from the traditional orange peel and coriander in Witbier to contemporary experiments with grapefruit and raspberries in IPAs. Like hops, these can be added during the boil, or during or after fermentation.

O **Final product** – The finished beer is then put into bottle, keg, can or cask as carefully as possible to avoid contamination, or ingress of oxygen, so that the beer can be enjoyed as the brewer intended.

## Tasting beer

There's a big difference between drinking and tasting. And there's a time and a place for both. There's nothing worse than someone giving you a full-blown analysis and description of a beer when you're trying to enjoy a chat at your local. However, if you want to expand your repertoire it helps to notice what you do and don't like about a beer, which requires more of a tasting approach. If you are studying beer for a qualification or for a professional reason there is a more formal process, but here we are assuming you are exploring for your own personal curiosity, when you can be more relaxed about it.

## Public service announcement

Session beers and the term 'sessionability' refer to beers that could be drunk over the course of an evening (or session). Although this is not an official term it mostly refers to beers with a lower alcohol level and refreshing palate.

## Do …

O **taste beers side by side.** It helps to be able to go back and forth between the beers, noticing the differences.

O **notice the appearance, smell, flavour and texture.** The taste experience of beer is a combination of all of these so it's worth noting what you like or dislike about each one.

O **sniff first, sip slowly, roll the beer around your mouth.** This helps you get the full experience. Notice what sensations and flavours are left after you've swallowed.

O **try and isolate the elements you are drawn to.** This enables you to explain to someone behind the bar or counter what you're looking for, so they can help you work out what are the right beers for you and point you to other beers with similar flavours or textures.

O **use good glasses.** If you're interested in getting the maximum flavour, use a tulip-shaped glass for tasting: they focus the aroma and direct it all to your nose and mouth. Pint glasses are possibly the worst 'vessel' for a tasting, but if that's what you've got, use that!

Don't ...

O **take it too seriously.** This is supposed to be fun! There is no right or wrong when it comes to your own tastes.

O **worry if you don't have the right words for the flavours.** When people learn to taste professionally they learn a code of flavours and words; if you haven't done this it's no surprise you don't know what 'biscuity' is as a flavour term. Instead use your own words, others will understand you.

O **think too hard about the flavours.** The harder you think the harder it gets to identify flavours and you'll start imagining them; instead just go with what you first experience. We're easily influenced too, so the second someone suggests a flavour you'll almost definitely taste it!

O **feel obliged to be clever or in the know.** Just notice for yourself what you do and don't like.

Kellerbier 🍺

Kölsch 🧭 🌐

Helles Lager 🍺

Radler 🌀

Premium European Lager Ⓢ

Pilsner 🍺

Märzen 🍺

Festbier 🌐
Open
Seasonally

Rauchbier 🌐

---

🍺 Production Method    Ⓢ Style    🧭 Starting point

🌀 Twist    🌐 Regional Speciality

# 1. Lager Line

Think you know lager? Think again. This line takes a journey through some of the beer world's purest, freshest, cleanest flavours that, when made well, sing from the glass and truly quench your thirst. The Lager Line goes from light and crisp Kellerbier through the intense apple and pear flavours of Pilsner to the deeper, rounder flavours of Märzen and Festbier and then on to the 'out there' smoky Rauchbier. You won't find heavy malt or lots of hops in any of these lagers, which makes them an all-round lighter option.

## When to take the Lager Line

When you're looking for an easy option that isn't too testing, or when you need something cool and light to refresh your palate.

## Stations on the Lager Line

Kellerbier, Kölsch, Helles Lager, Radler, Premium European Lager, Pilsner, Märzen, Festbier, Rauchbier.

# Kellerbier

Literally translating to 'cellar beer', this is the branch of the German lager family that is arguably the closest to 'natural' and as free from intervention as it gets.

**What you need to know:**

○ Kellerbiers in their truest form are unfined, unfiltered, unpasteurised, and served with only a slight natural carbonation. They tend to have a hop character (more so than other lagers) and a floral note which complements the bready notes from the yeast, which is preserved in suspension in the unfiltered beer and clouds the glass.

○ The beer is matured in unsealed (*ungespundet* in German, literally 'unbunged') wooden vats, the origin of the name Keller. As such, they will be more like traditional cask beer in appearance and carbonation than the typical effervescent lager. Without that high carbonation, they pour without the classic tight, fluffy, white head of a lager.

○ Kellerbiers are traditionally regarded as healthy in Germany and can be relied upon as a good source of vitamins – and if it's good enough for them …

○ As these beers were designed to be drunk directly from the cellar, and as fresh as possible, some examples are not truly authentic Kellerbier because a small amount of carbonation is added when bottled.

**Best enjoyed:**

To properly enjoy an authentic Kellerbier there's no better place to go than the Bräuhaus of one of the producers. Brewery-fresh, chilled wooden casks will be brought up from the cellar, tapped and dispensed right there. If not emptied within a couple of hours, the remainder of the cask will be ditched, and a fresh one brought up from the cellar, its arrival signalled by the ding of a bell behind the bar.

**Beers to look out for:**

Ayinger Kellerbier, Mönchshof Kellerbier, Sierra Nevada Keller Pils, Weihenstephaner 1516, St Georgen Bräu Kellerbier.

## Kölsch

A real wolf in sheep's clothing, a top-fermented ale capable of sneaking into a lager drinker's favourites.

**What you need to know:**

○ Golden in colour, bright, clear and divinely refreshing. Kölsch is fermented to the point that almost all the sugars are consumed, using a top-fermenting yeast that throws off juicy fruit aromas of apple and grape. This is then lagered (stored) cold for a short period of time to soften off any bold flavours and ensure your Kölsch is clean on the nose and totally thirst-quenching.

○ Although this should be very clean in flavour, you should expect German hops to take the lead here and contribute to the orchard fruit character, without being overly bitter.

○ In the late 1980s the Kölsch producers of the time lobbied the German state, and via the 'Kölsch Konvention' officially limited production to Köln (Cologne) and the surrounding region. Later, in the 1990s, Kölsch was granted Protected Geographical Indication by the EU. Despite this, other breweries in Germany, and a growing number overseas, are producing Kölsch-style beers, with various plays on words for their names.

**Best enjoyed:**
Kölsch beers have a natural affinity with cured pork and bread products, which makes it a great partner to one of those evenings where you graze a charcuterie board, or two, with a few friends and a lot of chat. The light acidity will balance the fat in the meats and the orchard fruit flavours are a great foil to the salt. If you want to make it feel a bit more authentic, serve in tall skinny 0.2 litre Kölsch glasses.

**Beers to look out for:**
Früh Kölsch, Thornbridge Tzara, Sion Kölsch, Gaffel Kölsch, Left Hand Travelin' Light.

## Helles Lager

For many in the industry this style represents the pinnacle of brewing talent: with no weird ingredients or heavy-handed dry hopping, there's nowhere to hide sloppy brewing.

**What you need to know:**
○ The term *Hell* simply means 'pale' in German. Any satanic association couldn't be further from the truth: Helles is crystal clear, and completely pure in character. There may be a slight whiff of sulphur when first poured, but this should dissipate quickly, leaving behind a beautifully clean nose, good fizz and flavours of spicy hops, hints of malt and a touch of sweet breadiness.
○ Coming from the Bavarian capital, Munich, Helles Lager is a very clear expression of beers brewed according to the *Reinheitsgebot* (the German laws regulating beer production). Pristine Munich water, world-famous German malted barley, herbaceous, spicy German hops, and a well-kept lager yeast are all that go into the making of Helles.

○ The temperature control during fermentation and a prolonged lagering period are essential to producing an excellent Helles, as the telltale butterscotch flavour of diacetyl which results from poor production is absolutely unacceptable in this style.

**Best enjoyed:**
The best place to enjoy Helles Lager is, by no small coincidence, also owned by the producers of the best example of the style. A warm day in the beer garden of the Augustiner Keller in central Munich is the perfect place to learn how to drink Helles. Take in a half-litre of Edelstoff, their export Helles dispensed straight from wooden casks, and enjoy the light carbonation of the world's most refreshing beer. A visit for lunch and dinner is essential too, so you can take your pick from the expansive menu of Bavarian classics.

**Beers to look out for:**
Augustiner Helles, Augustiner Edelstoff, Ayinger Lager Hell, Andechser Vollbier Hell, Tegernseer Hell, Thornbridge Lukas.

## Radler

Sometimes a drink is purely just a delicious refreshment. This branch line station is precisely that: juicy, low in alcohol, and with enough sweetness to revitalise.

**What you need to know:**
○ Radler is very specifically the 50/50 blend of Helles lager and traditional cloudy lemonade. As you can imagine, this blend is designed to be incredibly refreshing, bringing together an amazingly suppable beer style and reinvigorating lemonade.

- The name historically comes from a Munich landlord who had created a cycle path that led directly to his inn. On one particular day he was so overrun by cyclist guests, that to avoid running out of beer he created the *Radlermaß*, literally translating to cyclist's litre: by blending his remaining beer with lemonade he was able to stretch out his supply and make sure nobody went home thirsty.
- Although this is supposed to be a blend built from Helles and lemonade, the term has become abstracted to mean any beer blended back with a fruit soda, and it is now quite common to see Hefeweizens (wheat beers) used as the base beer. Several flavours are available, from the unsurprisingly refreshing grapefruit (of which the Schöfferhofer has become a beast of its own), all the way through to the peculiar flavouring of cactus. Go to a Bräuhaus and you may find a Dunkel Radler on offer, based on their Dunkel (dark) beer, and it is even possible to get a Cola blend too.

**Best enjoyed:**

Given its history, Radler is obviously an excellent post-sport refresher, but you can also take it as a base to have some real fun with. Having such a low alcohol level makes Radler a great background for experimenting with spirits. A grapefruit Radler with a shot of Mezcal added is an excellent pick-me-up, for those challenging mornings after.

**Beers to look out for:**

- Traditional – As mentioned above these are usually blended in bars and thus can't be found bottled in shops or bars.
- Non-traditional – Schöfferhofer Grapefruit, Stiegl Radler Grapefruit, Boulevard Ginger Lemon Radler.

# Premium European Lager

The beer that begins most people's beer journeys, whether it's Dutch, Italian, British or French. Ubiquitous around the world, especially when it comes to sport.

**What you need to know:**
- This station is a bit of a catch-all for the big-name lagers, served on draught and in bottles and cans around the world. The lagers all differ slightly, but share a refreshing, dry fizziness that is undeniably thirst-quenching.
- Most of these lagers are made at an industrial level and are often turned around very quickly with minimal lagering time, which can result in some off flavours in the final product. They also tend to use industrial versions of the natural ingredients used in smaller production beers, for example hop extract rather than whole leaf or pellet hops. This keeps the costs down but means the flavour is less interesting.
- Although most of these beers are now owned by big corporations, their origins are in local cultures. The breweries play on these local traditions in their marketing despite many of the beers no longer being produced in the original country.

**Best enjoyed:**
At a pavement café on a city break, after a long day of sightseeing. A cool beer and half an hour with the weight off your feet whilst watching the world go by will set you up for the next bit of your itinerary!

**Beers to look out for:**
Peroni Nastro Azzurro, Beck's, Estrella Damm, San Miguel, Moritz, Amstel, Mythos.

# Pilsner

Pilsner is one of the founding fathers of the lager dynasty, and as modern brewers take the style on a new wave of drinkers are enjoying this hoppy slant on lager.

What you need to know:

○ Technically, this station could be three or four substations, each with their own subtleties. The Pilsner station covers examples from the Czech Republic and Germany. The core characters of Pilsner remain a fresh, lager-style beer, with a more hop-focused flavour palate. The bright character of most of the Lager Line is obvious in Pilsner, as is the dry finish and refreshing carbonation.

○ Within the style the key difference is that German examples are drier and more bitter. Czech Pilsners are almost exclusively brewed with spicy Czech Saaz hops, whereas German examples use the more herbaceous German Hallertau.

○ The name Pilsner originates from the Czech town of Plzeň, where citizens in the mid 1800s outraged at poor-quality brewing took matters into their own hands. They built a brand new Bavarian-inspired brewery, and using Czech ingredients, and crucially, soft, slightly acidic Plzeň water, which extracts less harsh bitterness from the hops, and created a beer they could be proud of. This brewery went on to become the home of the world-famous Pilsner Urquell.

○ Although generally not a welcome flavour in lagers, rather divisively, diacetyl can be seen as a key component in Czech-style Pilsner, giving it a buttery character. This is largely a result of the yeast strain used.

Where better to enjoy Pilsner at its freshest than the Czech capital, Prague? From here you can make a Pilsner pilgrimage out to Plzeň and get a truly unique experience. Historically, Pilsner was matured in large wooden vats in cellars, and then transferred unfiltered and unpasteurised into smaller wooden casks for delivery to pub cellars. Only at the Pilsner Urquell brewery can you try this unique serve, which has a slightly more forceful bitterness but still retains that classic balance.

**Beers to look out for:**
- **Czech** – Pilsner Urquell, Staropramen, Budweiser Budvar.
- **German** – Berliner Pilsner, Victory Prima Pils, Birrificio Italiano Tipopils, Firestone Walker Pivo Pils.

## Märzen

A strong, amber lager, created as a loophole to an ancient brewing law, which occupies its own malty niche.

**What you need to know:**
- Märzen is a stronger amber lager that blends roasted malt flavours with some honey and toasty notes. Despite its darker colour it still has the freshness of lager and a touch of bitterness, which combine to create something flavoursome and refreshing.
- It came about thanks to a Bavarian royal decree in 1553 that banned brewing between the Feast of Saint George (April 23) and Michaelmas (September 29). Because of this decree, towards the end of March (thus the name Märzen) each year brewers would begin to produce stronger beers that were able to last this season in the rudimentary 'lagern' or cool storage caves.

○ Somewhat confusingly, much of what was originally exported to America as 'Oktoberfestbier' was in fact Märzen. The terms Oktoberfest and Festbier are reserved exclusively for the classic Munich breweries, but only within the EU, thus brewers from outside this select elite can brew a style fairly close to Festbier and get away with marketing it as such. Conversely, this has had the peculiar effect of many breweries in the US brewing Märzen and releasing it as their 'Festbier'.

### Best enjoyed:
A good option for when you're digging deep in lager land, but are not quite ready to move on to Doppelbock and the like. On that note, this makes a tremendous partner to Weisswurst, the traditional Bavarian boiled breakfast sausage, served with Bavarian sweet mustard. This pairing is no doubt absolute heresy to a Bavarian, who would insist that Weissbier is the only beer for Weisswurst, but is well worth a crack.

### Beers to look out for:
Ayinger Oktober Fest-Märzen, Flying Dog Dogtoberfest, Hacker-Pschorr Oktoberfest Märzen, Spaten Oktoberfest Ur-Märzen.

## Festbier

Stick a feather in your cap and don your Lederhosen or Dirndl. Oktoberfest comes round once a year, which is why this is a seasonal station, but it is such an enormous global phenomenon that this famous Munich style cannot be ignored.

What you need to know:

○ Festbier is produced by each of the six famous Munich breweries, but is also picked up by some American breweries, and a few others around Europe. Essentially a slightly stronger pale lager that has a little more malt character, it is effectively a punchier Helles.

○ American takes on the style are closer to Märzen, as the Festbiers designed for export (mostly to the US) were much more malt-driven, giving them a colour closer to amber.

○ Provenance is taken so seriously in Germany that Oktoberfestbier is actually a protected appellation within the EU that can strictly only be used by the breweries that are within the Munich city limits.

○ Oktoberfest actually takes place in September, with the last weekend traditionally being the first weekend in October. Originally it all happened in October, but it was eventually made longer and moved into September to take advantage of better weather.

○ A word that you will sometimes see associated with Festbier and Oktoberfest is Wiesn: this is not to be confused with Weizen. The term refers to the meadow where the festival is held each year, not the fact that these are wheat beers.

**Best enjoyed:**
There's no better way to experience this than to head over to Munich and experience Oktoberfest. See away a number of *Maß* (litre steins) and make the most of the funfair. Take care not to be rendered *ein Alkoholleiche*, literally translating to 'an alcohol corpse'.

**Beers to look out for:**
○ Augustiner Oktoberfestbier, Hacker-Pschorr Oktoberfest, Hofbräu Oktoberfestbier, Löwenbräu Oktoberfestbier, Paulaner Wiesn, Weihenstephaner Festbier.

## Rauchbier

Although this style is a member of the lager family, it takes the genre in a totally different and much smokier direction. Rauchbier is less about drinkability and more about layers of complex flavour that come in a deceptively easy-drinking format.

**What you need to know:**
○ The name directly translates to 'smoke beer' and that is exactly what you get. Most examples are neatly summed up by the phrase 'bacon in a glass': an overriding dry, smoky character built on top of a lager of very clean fermentation, which is very closely related to Märzen.
○ Rauchbier is the regional speciality of Bamberg in Bavaria. This city is surrounded by dense forests of beech trees, which were used as the fuel for the kilns in the city's maltings. These old-style kilns were directly fired, with the resulting beech smoke coming into contact with the wet malt, which would absorb all of the luxuriously toasty aromas from the smoke. Some of the breweries in the city

still have their own dedicated maltings working in the same way.

○ The aromas and flavours found in a good Rauchbier are the kind of things you'd be happy to find on a charcuterie board. Although significantly smoky, it shouldn't be overpowering, ashy in character, or taste like a fry-up gone wrong.

**Best enjoyed:**

It can be really fun to have a 'smoke off' between Rauchbier, peaty Islay whisky and even really wacky Riesling wine, to explore the different nuances in 'smoky' flavours and try to pull apart exactly what this means. Or why not try another flavour experiment and see if you can stack the smoke up against sour flavours to achieve a harmonious balance.

**Beers to look out for:**

Schlenkerla Rauchbier Märzen, Spezial Rauchbier, Schlenkerla Eiche, Yeastie Boys xeRRex, Yeastie Boys Rex Attitude.

Kölsch ◀ 🌐

Golden Ale ⚗

🍺 Blonde Ale ✳ - - ○ Fruit Beer Ⓢ

American Pale Ale ⚗

American IPA ◀ ⚗

White IPA ⚗

🍺 Belgian Blonde

Witbier ⚗

◎ Saison

Weissbier ⚗

Berliner Weisse 🌐

🌐 Tripel ○

Belgian Golden Strong Ale ⚗

---

🍺 Production Method    Ⓢ Style    ◀ Starting point

◎ Twist    🌐 Regional Speciality    ▥ Only open at weekends and bank holidays

# 2. Aromatic Line

If you like your beer to leap out of your glass and meet you before it hits your mouth, the Aromatic Line is for you. Beers on the Aromatic Line sit on the lighter side of the spectrum in terms of body, but not in flavour. If you travel the line you will encounter two of the most pungent styles of beer on your journey, the hoppy American IPA and fragrant wheat beers.

## When to take the Aromatic Line
When you are in need of refreshment. Beers on the Aromatic Line are all fresh, with a healthy dollop of carbonation which kick-starts the palate. Start at the northern end for lighter, drier styles which are less 'in-your-face' and then feel the intensity of the flavour increase as you travel down. The ales are perfect for watching the world go by and as you reach the bottom you come to the food-friendly Belgian beers, which will complement almost anything you eat with them.

## Stations on the Aromatic Line
Kölsch, Golden Ale, Blonde Ale, Fruit Beer, American Pale Ale, American IPA, White IPA, Belgian Blond, Saison, Witbier, Weissbier, Berliner Weisse, Belgian Golden Strong Ale, Tripel.

## Kölsch

*See Lager Line, p. 27.*

## Golden Ale

A Ronseal® of the beer world, Golden Ale does what it says on the tin, and is golden in both colour and nature.

**What you need to know:**

○ At the right time of year you'll also see Golden Ales referred to as Summer Ales, so as you can imagine these are finely balanced crushable pale ales. There will be a focus on hop character, usually American hops, but there is a good bready malt backbone too. Golden Ales lie somewhere between a classic Bitter and an American Pale Ale, with a key difference being the lower fizz level.

○ Golden Ales were key in helping CAMRA fight back against the rise of mass-produced lagers that were killing off Britain's brewing industry. Although served predominantly on cask, they were served at a lower temperature and targeted at the summertime refresher market.

○ The low carbonation levels of Golden Ale mean they are a great gateway beer for anybody looking to make the move from lager styles to cask ales and vice versa for Bitter (see p. 78) drinkers to make a move towards more flavourful ale styles.

**Best enjoyed:**
Given its versatility and name, Golden Ale is a great beer to have at a summer party or gathering. It should appeal to both lager and other ale drinkers, whilst being soft enough not to put anyone off. All you need is a barbecue and swingball and you're sorted.

**Beers to look out for:**
Moor Nor' Hop, Moor So' Hop, Dark Star Hophead, Cromarty Hit the Lip, Fyne Avalanche, Brooklyn Summer Ale, Oakham JHB.

## Blonde Ale

A fantastic entry point to the world of ale for a beer newbie, or a great crossover opportunity for lager drinkers to expand their palates. Ultimately sessionable, generally available at a wallet-friendly price, and usually at a fairly low ABV.

**What you need to know:**
- Blonde ale is a bridging point between American Pale Ale and lager. It has the same fruity hop character as APA but loses some of the bitterness, instead having a breadier, maltier flavour.
- Some brewers use lager or Kölsch yeasts to ensure they create a very clean fermentation, with minimal yeast character.
- It was originally developed in brewpubs as an alternative to producing lager. This was generally done by those that didn't have the tank space or lagering time to devote to easy-drinking, clean lager styles.

**Best enjoyed:**
Typically best enjoyed in large quantities, over a long period of time, in a sunny, grassy beer garden. An excellent companion to pub grub fish and chips, as many bar kitchens will use the house blonde ale to make their batter with. On a more specific note, Fyne Jarl is best used to keep you going during 'Fynefest', hosted at the brewery on the banks of Loch Fyne each year. A music festival, featuring incredible local beer, oysters and salmon at it.

**Beers to look out for:**
Fyne Jarl, Fallen Odyssey, Victory Summer Love.

## Fruit Beer

A great starting point for someone who has a sweet tooth, or lovers of flavoured cider. It is also a winner on hot days when you want the equivalent of a beer ice lolly.

**What you need to know:**
O Most fruit beers add fruit pulp or essence to a beer, so you get a big dollop of the fruit flavour and an undertone of the beer character. The most common are stone fruits like peach and apricot or soft fruits like raspberry. Fruit beers tend to be sweet with a hint of savoury or dry from the beer. More often than not, these beers are flavoured with artificial ingredients, which can lead to them having amped-up aromas that really hammer home which fruit they are supposed to represent. This can make them a bit 'cartoon' in character, so you may want to move on to something a bit more subtle after a pint or two.

- The beer in fruit beer can vary; this is generally represented in the name, i.e. Raspberry Wheat, or Peach Pale Ale. It is worth noting that many breweries are now producing fruited sour ales, which can be a great step into a new world of beer.
- Fruit Beer is generally considered simple, and should not be confused with the more layered and serious Fruit Lambic style (see p. 112). Although not neighbours on the BeerTubeMap, a trip to Fruit Lambic would open up a lot of different options to a Fruit Beer fan.

**Best enjoyed:**
Chilled, down on the beach in guilty-pleasure mode; think of it as your beer Solero* (other ice creams are available). For many beer drinkers fruit beers are too sweet, but on a hot day with your feet in the sand even the most sniffy of drinkers would welcome a couple of these fruity numbers.

**Beers to look out for:**
Samuel Smith's (Various), Buxton Trolltunga (Sour), Buxton/Omnipollo Lemon Meringue Ice Cream Pale, Tiny Rebel Clwb Tropicana.

## American Pale Ale

This is the modern 'craft' drinkers' equivalent to the 'lawnmower beer'. Fresh, juicy, dry, and readily crushable. For many, this is the first choice for a post-work beer.

**What you need to know:**
- This is the first port of call for anybody looking to develop a taste for hoppy beer. Generally crisp and dry, with a light biscuit style, the main flavouring is left to the hop.

Depending on the variety used, the flavours can range from mildly floral and grassy all the way through to intense tropical fruit.

O APA has become the basis to show off a single hop variety, which in turn has brought knowledge and preferences for particular hop varietals to the average drinker. You now see the hop variety name – for example Citra or Mosaic – on the bottle to denote the flavour profile, and sometimes the hop variety is the beer's full name.

O All about aroma, APAs are typically heavily late-hopped in the boil, and given a good dry-hopping after fermentation.

O They are generally pale in colour, but some examples will stray towards amber, with a touch of crystal malt used to add depth to the colour.

O APAs have their roots with the American homebrewers of the 1980s, who initially developed them whilst replicating classic recipes from the UK using American ingredients found in their homebrew stores. In a curious twist of history, this has gone on to be one of the most widely produced styles by modern UK craft breweries.

**Best enjoyed:**
Open your weekend with a drink that matches your intentions: vibrant, easy-going and full of glorious flavour. It's that first beer that doesn't even have a chance to touch the sides. Or geek it up by taste-testing in a nerdy session of trying to pick apart characteristics of different hop varieties.

**Beers to look out for:**
The Kernel Pale Ale (various hops), Beavertown Gamma Ray, Track Sonoma, Sierra Nevada Pale, Oakham Citra, Northern Monk Faith.

# American IPA

In modern 'craft' beer terms this is the widely brewed style that launched an entire flavour revolution in beer.

**What you need to know:**

○ American IPA is the true home station of any hophead. Built to be extremely bitter and extremely aromatic, these beers are usually dosed with an enormous charge of American hops. You should expect deep resinous notes, sticky pine, and a rasping bitterness, all weighed up against punchy New World hop aromas of citrus pith, and even a herbal character often linked to marijuana (a close cousin of the humble hop).

○ Although labelled here for simplicity as American IPA, there is a distinction to be made between East Coast and West Coast styles. East Coast-style IPAs will express a little more balance, with a touch more malt, in comparison to the all-out hoppiness on the West Coast.

○ However, New England-style IPA has begun to spread beyond the leafy north-east. This new substyle is focused on extremes of flavour and aroma, at the sacrifice of clarity and appearance, producing beers that are full of flavour but extremely cloudy and murky in the glass. Despite this peculiar new look, they have a tendency to be delicious. Many of them are made at breweries who sell almost all of their stock straight from the brewery door to long lines of thirsty customers.

○ Although there were others before it, San Diego's Stone Brewing's IPA, produced in 1997, is credited with kick-starting the modern world's love affair with American IPA. Their preference for intense bitterness sparked a race for brewers to create the beer with the highest IBU (International Bitterness Unit) level, which in turn led to developments in brewing techniques to make more flavoursome IPA.

**Best enjoyed:**
Young and fresh! Despite its distinct, hoppy flavour American IPA has captured the hearts, and tastebuds, of thousands who can't get enough of its herbaceous, bitter notes. These deteriorate from the minute they develop so you should always check the date on your label and buy the youngest you can.

**Beers to look out for:**
Stone IPA, Lagunitas IPA, Magic Rock Cannonball, The Kernel IPA (various), Thornbridge Huck, Redchurch Great Eastern IPA, Fallen Platform C, Tempest Brave New World, Cromarty AKA IPA, Buxton Axe Edge.

## White IPA

This hard-to-find style should be more popular than it is, balancing the freshness of IPA with the flavours of Witbier. From here the line forks towards the banana of Belgian styles or the floral and orange flavours of wheat-based beers.

**What you need to know:**
○ White IPA is a challenging style to properly balance. Good examples should have a bitterness close to an American-style IPA but without the resinous flavours associated with it; these combine with delicate notes of orange peel and jasmine, which should win out against the hop-associated aromas.

○ This is a style that popped up in the mid-2010s, but is now very seldom seen. As such it hasn't truly had a chance to be properly defined. In essence, it is an IPA built with the flavours typically found in Witbier. These flavours can be imparted either through the use of spices and adjuncts, or through fermentation with a Witbier yeast strain.

O It's a fantastic segue from Weissbier to IPA and the other way, particularly for people who find the bitterness of IPA a bit too much.

**Best enjoyed:**
This is a bit of a tough one to find as not many breweries give it a go. However, the delicate floral flavours and balance make for a good match for aromatic food, as long as it isn't too spicy. Try it in a tulip glass with some Thai-style starters.

**Beers to look out for:**
Two Roads Honeyspot Road, De Dochter van de Korenaar Crime Passionnel, Cromarty Whiteout, New Belgium Accumulation.

## Belgian Blond

Although mostly famed for punchy Trappist styles, Belgium's contribution to the world of session drinking should not be overlooked. Belgian Blond is classically dry and drinkable, with just a hint of some interesting flavours created by the fermentation.

**What you need to know:**
O Belgian Blond is a great Goldilocks session beer. Imagine the fresh, orchard flavours of a golden ale, with an interesting layer of orange and foam banana over the top of it. It makes for a great, long drink.

- The 'Belgian' part is down to the yeast used, which creates those banana ester flavours, but these are just part of a fresher, fruitier ale-style beer. If you're not a fan of full-on wheat beer, this is a good midway point.
- The 'blond' label can often be a source of confusion, as it is referred to as Blond in Belgium, Blonde in France, and nothing like what we would perceive as a Blonde ale in the UK. To confuse matters further, occasionally some Trappist beers are labelled as Blond too. To be sure you're at the right station, look for Belgian Blond on the label to differentiate it.
- At the most basic level, Belgian Blonds are more drinkable, lower in ABV, and less bitter than Tripel and Belgian Golden Strong Ales, making them the perfect Belgian session ale.

**Best enjoyed:**
Bruges is undoubtedly the best place to enjoy Belgian Blond, where noted producer Brugse Zot have famously constructed a beer pipeline under the streets of Bruges, to save their tankers having to drive the 3.2km journey through winding medieval streets from their brewery to their packaging plant.

**Beers to look out for:**
Brugse Zot Blond, Westvleteren Blond, De La Senne Brussels Calling, De Ranke XX Bitter.

## Saison

Saison is a style with a fairly loose concept of what it should be. If you're trying to nail down the flavour of funk, this is an excellent starting point.

**What you need to know:**

O Saison was originally the product of farmhouses in Belgium and France, designed to refresh seasonal workers. It is a light and generally low-ABV sessionable beer, which is dry as a bone, with a sour note and some hop bitterness. However, due to its historically very loosely controlled fermentation there is significant complexity and aroma in Saison. The yeast used will typically express quite a peppery character, but many examples will lean very closely to the phenolic side, giving a rustic, spicy, almost Tripel-like quality.

O Given their farmhouse origins, Saisons would typically have been of mixed fermentation, with multiple strains of yeast and even some bacteria at play. It is very much a 'kitchen sink' beer style and a wide variety of grains and other adjuncts can be found in Saisons. Spelt, oats, wheat and rye are not uncommon, and each tweaks the flavour.

O Additionally, Saisons were often flavoured with whatever seasonal ingredients were around at the time, a practice that is still continued, with many breweries using a Saison as the background for experimenting with weird adjunct combinations. If you can eat it, somebody's probably made a Saison with it.

**Best enjoyed:**
If ever there was a beer style made to enjoy with cheese, Saison is it. This is not fancy cheeseboard territory, you need to keep it rustic. Chunks of fresh crusty bread, preferably torn by hand,

with a thick wedge of cheese hastily thumbed in to create a simple ploughman's. Ideally you want to try and match the funk of your cheese up against the funk of your Saison, so go for farmhouse, raw milk styles if you can.

Beers to look out for:
Saison Dupont, Fantôme Saison, Boulevard Tank 7, Burning Sky Saison La Provision, Burning Sky Saison Anniversaire, The Kernel Bière de Saison.

## Witbier

A flavoured quencher with plenty of depth, a hint of orange and a creamy texture.

What you need to know:
○ Imagine a cross between Weissbier, Tripel and Belgian Blond, with a bit of fruit and spice thrown in for good measure. Witbier has a distinct orange and coriander flavour with a creamy texture and hints of banana and bubblegum. It is extremely refreshing and often served with a slice of orange.
○ Witbier is produced with a grist of as much as 50 per cent unmalted wheat, and many of the flavours you taste are added elements. It is spiced with Curaçao orange peel, coriander and occasionally grains of paradise. The final beers will still be dry in finish, but considerably juicier than a Belgian Blond Ale. Some examples will show a slight lactic tartness.
○ Witbier was all but extinct in the 1960s, until Pierre Celis effectively resurrected the style by developing Hoegaarden in 1965 at the new Celis brewery. After a period of rapid expansion, his brewery unfortunately burned down and in

1985 he was forced to sell part of the business to Stella Artois. The business then went through a series of mergers and acquisitions during which decisions were made based on spreadsheets rather than quality. So in 1990 he stepped away, although the brand continues.

**Best enjoyed:**
Watching the world go by: whether it's at a pavement café or the base of a ski-resort, a glass of Witbier will quench your thirst. The mix of flavours is better than most cheap, frothy lagers, and the creamy texture will fill you up until the next pitstop.

**Beers to look out for:**
St Bernardus Blanche, Fantôme Blanche, Magic Rock Clown Juice, Celis Wit, Allagash White, Hoegaarden.

## Weissbier

An acquired taste, but one that has been going since the Middle Ages and has become a favourite worldwide.

**What you need to know:**
○ On paper a highly carbonated, cloudy beer tasting of bananas and cloves sounds like something to be given a bodyswerve. However, this flavour sensation has become a worldwide favourite. Weissbier is a world-famous speciality originating from Bavaria in the Middle Ages. The amazing thing is that these flavours are produced solely by the yeast during fermentation, rather than by addition of adjuncts. Weissbier yeast will throw off esters reminiscent of banana and bubblegum, which are balanced up against the almost smoky clove phenols.

- Weissbiers are generally served cloudy, as most of the incredible flavour in them is related to the yeast. If you filter out the yeast, you run the risk of filtering out this flavour too. Additionally, a bit of yeast is a good source of vitamins, something that a lot of German brands play heavily upon.
- Wheat can be a challenging grain to brew with as, unlike barley, it does not have a thick husk, and when used in high concentrations can cause issues with run-off from the mash tun. Wheat is also particularly high in protein, and it is these long-chain proteins that help to build its characteristic long-lasting white fluffy head.
- As the *Reinheitsgebot* only stated water, barley and hops as the key ingredients of beer, the private breweries at the time were not allowed to brew Weissbier. For over three centuries Weissbier could only be produced by ducal decree (as long as it was top-fermented) and Hofbräu enjoyed exclusivity on this style up until 1872, when the rise of bottom-fermented lagers, now tasting consistently excellent thanks to the invention of refrigeration, caused them to abandon the production. After an appeal to the court of King Ludwig II of Bavaria, Georg Schneider (of Schneider Weisse fame) became the first commoner granted the right to produce Weissbier.

**Best enjoyed:**
The distinctive banana flavour of Weissbier is definitely an acquired taste, so once you've acquired it why not double down and serve it with pancakes topped with banana and maple syrup instead of a prosecco brunch? The smooth texture of the beer will complement the doughy pancakes and the banana in the beer will be emphasised by the banana topping. Pure indulgence.

**Beers to look out for:**
Schneider Weisse Unser Original Tap 7, Weihenstephaner Hefeweissbier, Erdinger Weissbier, Ayinger Bräu-Weisse, Andechser Weissbier Hell, Maisel's Weisse.

## Berliner Weisse

A beer with a new lease of life! American and European craft breweries are rekindling a passion for this traditional German beer and reshaping it. This is an unlikely intersection on the BeerTubeMap which opens up lots of flavour opportunity, but only if you get that far.

**What you need to know:**
○ Essentially, Berliner Weisse is a low ABV wheat-based beer, soured with *Lactobacillus* giving it a tart, creamy tang on the finish. It is traditionally served with a splash of either Woodruff, Raspberry, or plain sugar syrup, and occasionally Caraway Schnapps in order to offset the sour finish.
○ The Berliner Weisse style has now been picked up by modern craft breweries as a blank canvas for throwing different fruits and herbs at, which create wacky flavour combinations evolving the idea of beer and syrup further.
○ The sourness in Berliner Weisse should be lactic rather than acetic, giving it a creamy tang. Bad examples can suffer from a butyric acid aroma (baby sick), or be overly acidic, rather than gently refreshing and drinkable.
○ Similar strains of *Lactobacillus* used to ferment Berliner Weisse can be found in natural yoghurt, and some brewers will actually sour their Berliner wort by pitching yoghurt straight into it. However, both methods are routes to the same end, being more about brewer preference than the end result.

○ It is not always easy to find straight examples of Berliner Weisse, and it is changing all the time, so you may need to get your Sherlock hat on to track it down.

**Best enjoyed:**
A straight Berliner Weisse makes for an incredible summer cooler. Think homemade cloudy lemonade, but with a tiny lick of booze. Alternatively, flavoured Berliner Weisse is a great opportunity to have fun with food pairing. Counter it with a sweet dessert, or use it to try and highlight a flavour within a dish.

**Beers to look out for:**
○ **Unflavoured** – Berliner Kindl Weisse, The Kernel London Sour, Stone Berlin White Ghost.
○ **Flavoured** – Mad Hatter Tzatziki Sour, Siren Calypso.

## Belgian Golden Strong Ale

These are the beers that stealthily sneak up on you when on holiday in Belgium for the first time. A bit of a contradiction in terms, these are deceptively punchy in ABV and dangerously refreshing.

**What you need to know:**
○ At the most fundamental level, Belgian Golden Strong Ales are very closely related to Tripels (see p. 56). The key difference between Belgian Golden Strong and Tripel is that it is fermented with yeast strains that produce more fruit-led phenols, rather than the spicy character that Tripel is so famous for. With telltale flavours of pears and orange, high alcohol and a hint of spice, it's more of a crowd-pleaser than you might think.

- The refreshing nature of Belgian Golden Strong Ale is due to the fermentations that finish dry rather than leaving some sweetness, and the fact that it typically has high carbonation, giving a pleasant prickle on the palate. Many of them undergo a primary fermentation, before additional yeast and dextrose are added, to continue to dry out the finished beer.
- The yeast strain used by Duvel, to create what is arguably the benchmark of this style, was originally harvested from a McEwan's Scotch Ale after the First World War. This strain is still used to this day. Although original versions of the beer were slightly dark, it was eventually reinterpreted to be brewed pale in colour, as the fashions and tastes of the time moved towards Pilsner-style beers.

**Best enjoyed:**
The Belgian classic beef stew, Carbonnade Flamande, is traditionally made with something dark and rich from the Trappist range of styles, however, subbing in a Belgian Golden Strong Ale like Delirium Tremens gives this heart-warming beef stew a whole new dimension. Once you've left your Carbonnade to simmer for about an hour or so the beer contributes an intriguing bitterness.

**Beers to look out for:**
Duvel, Delirium Tremens, Dulle Teve, Piraat, Brooklyn Local 1.

## Tripel

The most widely consumed of the classic Trappist styles, despite its reasonably punchy ABV. This pale classic plays a spicy foil to the fruity Belgian Golden Strong Ales.

**What you need to know:**

○ Tripels are all about spicy phenols produced during fermentation. Zippy spiced notes of white pepper, burnt orange peel and lemongrass are commonly found, against a backdrop of honey flavours but without the honey sweetness: the finish is dry. Refined examples will belie their punchy ABV, typically in the region of 8–9%.

○ Bitterness in Tripels can be fairly high, in comparison to similar Belgian styles, but this is often balanced out by the flavours produced during fermentation, and their inherent booziness. Some light candi sugar and sucrose is added to achieve the high ABV, but simultaneously ensure a very dry finish to the beer.

○ The name, pronounced trip-ell and not triple, was historically first used by Westmalle in 1956 in reference to the strongest beer they had made, originally produced as Superbier in 1933. It allegedly also refers to the fact that three times the malt was required to brew a Tripel, in comparison to the Trappist 'Single' beer.

**Best enjoyed:**

Tripel is a beer worthy of a bit of respect, it has history, complexity, a delicious range of flavours and you don't need much to feel the effects. So why not make a toast with it, whether you're wetting a baby's head or celebrating a special birthday, it's a great glass charger!

**Beers to look out for:**
Westmalle Tripel, Brugse Zot Tripel, Tripel Karmeliet, Dupont
Avec Les Bon Voeux, Chimay White Cap, Het Anker Gouden
Carolus Tripel, La Rulles Triple.

Märzen 🍺

Altbier 🍺 🌐

Extra Special Bitter 🍺
(ESB)

Old Ale 🍺

Red Ale 🍺

Amber Ale 🍺

British IPA 🍺

American IPA 🍺 ➤

Double IPA Ⓢ

Dry Hop Sour ◎

Gose 🌐

Berliner Weisse 🌐

---

  Production Method  Ⓢ Style  ➤ Starting point

◎ Twist  🌐 Regional Speciality

# 3. Discovery Line

The Discovery Line is for the adventurous palate, looking for something a bit different. It encompasses beers with a malty edge, starting with Märzen and Altbier, and ends up on a tangy, sour note with Gose and Berliner Weisse. In the middle you find beers that have a Goldilocks intensity, neither too heavy nor too light, and an interesting palate of flavours starting malty and getting hoppier as you go.

## When to take the Discovery Line
When you want a beer with some interesting flavours that are a bit more off the beaten track. The Discovery Line is less about pure refreshment: you'll find something interesting in every mouthful.

## Stations on the Discovery Line
Märzen, Altbier, Extra Special Bitter (ESB), Old Ale, Red Ale, Amber Ale, British IPA, American IPA, Double IPA, Dry Hop Sour, Gose, Berliner Weisse.

## Märzen

*See Lager Line, p. 33.*

## Altbier

Altbier is the dangerously drinkable, copper-coloured regional speciality of Düsseldorf that straddles the boundary between lager and ale.

**What you need to know:**

O Altbier is typically malty and slightly sweet, but this sweetness is balanced against a dose of classic European hop varieties to provide bitterness and spice.

O Altbier is fermented with an ale yeast at warm temperatures, but lagered for eight weeks at −2°C to +5°C. This fermentation produces lower levels of esters, and the lagering allows the yeast to reabsorb most of them and other potential off-flavours, to produce a very clean-tasting beer.

O Like many classic European styles, the First and Second World Wars vastly reduced the number of producers: there were once in excess of 100 producers in the Düsseldorf area, but now it only has four independent Altbier breweries.

O Keep an eye out for stronger '*Sticke*' versions (meaning secret or whisper in regional dialect), these are brewed very occasionally, and historically only advertised by a sign that read 'Sticke tomorrow'.

**Best enjoyed:**
Given it is the regional speciality, Düsseldorf is the quintessential Altbier destination. Take a seat in one of the brewpubs and sit back as your *Köbe* (Bräuhaus waiter) keeps a steady flow of the distinctive, skinny, 0.2 litre glasses that Altbier is served in coming your way. They will make a tally on your beer mat each time until you place the mat on top of your glass, to show that you have had enough. *Schweinshaxe*, roasted pork knuckle, usually covered in dangerously crispy crackling, makes an excellent companion to the beer.

**Beers to look out for:**
Uerige Alt, Füchschen Alt, Kürzer Alt, Schlösser Alt.

## Extra Special Bitter (ESB)

A truly traditional British style that was taken on and popularised by many of the early US brewpubs. Due to this, the style can sometimes be split into UK and US styles.

**What you need to know:**
○ For brewers this is a fantastic opportunity to display a deft hand with malty flavours, a very earthy English hop character, and an overriding glorious marmalade-on-toast vibe, captured in a pint glass. A lot of the character found in these styles comes from the use of English ale yeasts that finish quite dry but provide a hedgerow fruit character. Some brewers in the United States give this style a twist by using American hops, making it more like grapefruit marmalade on toast.

- One difficulty with this style, particularly in the UK, is that the majority of the volume is produced by large regional brewers, many of whom bottle in clear glass bottles. Sadly, the beer inside is affected by UV light, causing a distinctive flavour fault known as skunking, when alpha acids from the hops break down and react with the hydrogen sulphide produced by the yeast. As the name suggests, this is a nasty aroma, apparently similar to that produced by a skunk, also similar to burning tyres or a tomcat's spray.
- ESB often has a touch of butterscotch on the palate, which is down to a fermentation by-product, diacetyl. Although this is relatively acceptable in this style of beer because of the English ale yeasts used, badly managed it can end up as a fault, with a rancid butter taste. However, this shouldn't happen with high-quality producers.
- The term ESB is wholly owned by Fuller's in the UK, but many brewers further afield release beers under this name and style.

**Best enjoyed:**
There can be no doubt that the best way to enjoy an ESB is on cask in a proper traditional English pub, log fire ablaze, perhaps even indulging in the Sunday roast. On the topic of a Sunday roast, kick-start your gravy with plenty of beer, lashings of butter, onions, stock and seasoning.

**Beers to look out for:**
Fuller's ESB, SKA ESB Special Ale, Moor/Fuller's Relentless Optimism, Adnams Broadside.

# Old Ale

A dark, very British tradition that elusively appears on annual release or in the dark of the winter.

**What you need to know:**

○ Old Ale is a dark(ish) beer that blends the maltiness of traditional British brewing, with the tanginess of dark fruit and the spice of English hops. It can vary in colour, with the darker versions having more leather, tobacco and malt on the palate as a result of the beer being matured on wood. It is traditionally between 4% and 6% ABV, so is an interesting darker beer to be drinking in pint-sized servings.

○ Old Ale originated during the Industrial Revolution, when the beer was aged in open-topped wooden tuns and was often used as a 'stock ale' to blend back in to balance beers produced in summer that could suffer faults due to a lack of refrigeration. Whilst you wouldn't want to be drinking the ale as it was then, it is the tuns and the bacteria populations living in the wood, that to this day are used to contribute a hint of funk or tartness.

○ Theakston Old Peculier is probably the best known of the Old Ales available, and without Theakston and a couple of other breweries championing the style it may well have disappeared. However, Old Peculier and many other commercial examples are not matured in wood, and thus don't have the distinct flavours that others brewed by smaller brewers do.

○ Majority Ale is a sub-style of Old Ale that used to be produced to celebrate the birth of a child. However, unlike the tradition of cracking something open to celebrate the wetting of a baby's head, Majority Ale was aged until it was drunk on the child's twenty-first birthday.

Old Ale tends to appear as bottled beer, so when you do find it in cask it can be quite an event. This is CAMRA territory, so head to the *Good Beer Guide* to find the best real ale pub in your neighbourhood, where you can guarantee all the cask ale will be at its peak. Go the whole hog and take a book or the paper and take your time over a pint.

**Beers to look out for:**
Fuller's Vintage Ale, Theakston Old Peculier, Brains The Rev James, Moor Fusion, Moor Old Freddy Walker.

## Red Ale

A station undergoing renovation, from its malty Irish origins to a more hop-driven New World style.

**What you need to know:**

○ Red Ale gets its name, unsurprisingly, from its red hue, a result of the extended kilning the malt is given. The prolonged kilning of the malt has a dual result: it gives a sweet biscuit character on the nose, but the kilning also lowers the diastatic power of the malt, resulting in a less fermentable and thus slightly sweeter beer. Red Ale is a balancing act between sweet, dry and bitter and has a tinge of berry and tea flavours, which are offset by the grassy dose of hops.

○ Like Bitter, the use of hops is evident in Red Ale but their spicy, green notes are used to balance the beer rather than overpower it, resulting in an easy-drinking session ale. These two stations can be considered cousins of sorts.

○ However, unlike Bitter, Red Ale has been claimed by the new wave of brewing, both in the UK and the US, and this has resulted in an evolution of the style. Modern Red Ales tend to be drier, with a bigger focus on the citrus and grapefruit characteristics of American hops. This results in a beer with a bit more bite, and as is often the case with modern ales, a bit more alcohol.

**Best enjoyed:**
If Amber Ale is your go-to summer pint, Red Ale is its wintry equivalent: that extra dose of flavour means the beer doesn't have to be so cold in the glass to still be refreshing. Good for Saturday afternoon catch-ups when you're just whiling away the time.

**Beers to look out for:**
Thornbridge Colorado Red, Fourpure Flatiron, Tiny Rebel Cwtch, Magic Rock Rapture.

## Amber Ale

Amber Ale showcases the delicate balance between the vivid flavour and aroma of American hops and a pronounced biscuity malt character. However, modern examples tend to lean to one or other side of the balance.

**What you need to know:**
- Amber Ale is a great beer to explore typical American hop characteristics; you should taste a refreshing dose of resin flavours and citrus peel, stacked up against caramel and crystal malt flavours.
- It is a relatively young style, appearing towards the end of the twentieth century alongside the advent of American craft breweries.

○ It is named, unsurprisingly, after its amber appearance, with some examples approaching copper. Balance is key here, and should be neither overly bitter nor too sweet and malty. It can be dry-hopped for additional aroma. The malt flavour should ideally be biscuit and caramel, rather than roasty or chocolatey.

**Best enjoyed:**
A great style for watching over the transition from summer to autumn. The bright American hop character refreshes and makes the most of an Indian summer, while the malt character reminds you that the leaves on the trees are beginning to turn, and you should probably dig out that favourite scarf.

**Beers to look out for:**
Wiper and True Amber, Tempest Face With No Name, Hitachino Nest Amber Ale, Modern Times Blazing World.

## British IPA

The difference between British and American IPAs is an important distinction to make. The rise of the American-style IPA means the very high quality British-style IPAs are misunderstood and their flavours dismissed for not being aromatic or bitter enough.

**What you need to know:**
- This is a style that properly focuses on the best of British, showing off the high-quality malted barley produced on these isles, and when done right it can pull incredible levels of flavour out of UK hops that are traditionally thought of as twiggy and boring.
- What you're looking for here is a spicier, more pepper-like hop profile, rather than the resinous and citrusy profiles offered by American and New World IPA examples. Keep an eye out for Jester hopped beers, which should bring a pithy marmalade character; Jester is a UK-grown hop, which is a close relative of the immensely popular American Cascade hop.
- These beers are said to be representative of those sent by boat to India, that sparked the oft-debated IPA origin myth. Despite IPA's reputation for strength and bitterness, research has shown that beers known as IPA produced in England at that time were weaker and less bitter than their pale ale contemporaries.

**Best enjoyed:**
In a world where the US brewers dominate, it's good to celebrate our native British hops. There's nowhere better to do this than the Kentish coast for some old-school seaside revival. In the nineteenth century, tens of thousands of city-weary families from London's East End would spend their holidays

picking hops in the fresh air of Kent. Whilst you might not want to go hop-picking as a holiday, Margate and Ramsgate are treading the fine line between gentrification and traditional seafront. So head to the cutting-edge Turner gallery in Margate for some culture and then sit on the sea front eating local oysters washed down with some British IPA.

**Beers to look out for:**
Moor Return of the Empire, Fuller's Bengal Lancer, Birra Del Borgo ReAle, Tryst Raj IPA, Swannay Orkney IPA.

## American IPA

*See Aromatic Line, p. 45.*

## Double IPA Ⓢ

If you love IPA, this is the next logical step, bringing everything that IPA has but even bigger.

**What you need to know:**
○ Double the flavour, usually double the quantity of hops, and quite often double the ABV of a regular IPA. Double IPAs, known as DIPAs, tend to be dry and highly aromatic, with all focus being on the bitter, grapefruit herbaceousness of the hop flavour.
○ This is a station in development, the rules are less fixed for DIPA: the method of doubling the flavour can differ, and is trend-dependent. For a while it was a race for the highest IBUs; maximising the hop aroma was the trend at other times; of late, breweries have been experimenting with ways

to utilise different yeast strains to get the most out of the style. All of this results in breweries turning out new versions all the time and creating a rush for the latest DIPA.

○ This 'craze' sees beer fans queue for hours at breweries for a handful of cans, or crashing website servers on release day to catch the latest raft of releases.

○ In fact modern DIPAs have also been immensely popular with tickers and traders, an unofficial network of people buying up and swapping the small-batch multiple releases produced every month by new-wave breweries. These swapsies reach a highly engaged group of enthusiasts across the Atlantic and Europe.

○ The resurgence in interest in DIPAs, and brewers' insistence that they be drunk as fresh as possible, has prompted amazing developments in the supply chain, with importers and wholesalers investing heavily in speed of transit and cold chain transport facilities.

**Best enjoyed:**
This style has arguably benefited the most from the return of canning as the premium packaging method for maintaining freshness and quality. As such a DIPA (kept cool in your backpack) is the perfect way to celebrate summiting your local peak on a blazing hot day. Given the current focus on aroma, DIPAs also make a great partner to aromatic foods, but any chilli heat should be avoided.

**Beers to look out for:**
Cloudwater (new DIPAs released regularly), Northern Monk (various), Thornbridge Halcyon, Brew By Numbers 55/ (various), Alchemist Heady Topper, Cromarty Man Overboard.

## Dry Hop Sour

A relatively modern development, not yet fully recognised as a style but fairly widely produced. The beer equivalent of Haribo Tangfastics, this style takes tangy to a new level.

**What you need to know:**

O Dry Hop Sour is a style that provides two real flavour extremes, smashing together acidic sour beer, and extremely fragrant hops. This gives the drinker a huge burst of flavour up front and then a mouth-watering more-ishness when the acidity hits. They probably aren't the beer for a session as the acidity and sharpness can tire the palate.

O They are usually produced by the 'kettle souring' method, where wort is collected into the kettle and held overnight at a temperature that favours fermentation by *Lactobacillus* strains (around 44°C) to give it the sour character. This can then be boiled along with hops, and cast into the fermenter for the fermentation to be finished by a conventional ale yeast, before a generous dry-hopping to give the aroma.

O Other brewers boil the wort with a small amount of hops before souring in the kettle, to allow the *Lactobacillus* culture to survive and take care of the fermentation. This is trickier as too many alpha acids or oils from the hops in the boil will stop the *Lactobacillus* from doing its job. Both methods result in a similar flavour in the final beer, so the choice of production method is down to the brewer's preferences.

O Similar to Berliner Weisse, badly managed souring practices can result in deeply unpleasant off flavours such as the baby sick flavours of butyric acid.

**Best enjoyed:**
Given that dry-hopped sours are typically clean in flavour, and more focused on aroma, it can be quite fun to use them as a palate cleanser in a multi-course beer dinner, the same way you would use a sorbet.

**Beers to look out for:**
Chorlton Brewery (various), Lervig Hop Drop Sour, Redchurch Urban Farmhouse Dry Hop Sour, Mikkeller Spontandryhop, Crooked Stave Hop Savant.

## Gose

Another beer style that came within inches of extinction, but is now a firmly established style in the modern 'craft' scene. Gose is a perplexing contrast of acidity, salinity and thorough refreshment.

**What you need to know:**
○ Gose is salty, which sounds odd for a beer, but it is true. This was originally due to the naturally salty river water used in the production process, but now the salt is added to the brewing water. This saltiness combines with a tart, citrus acidity and some greener herbal notes to create the ultimate quencher, albeit not to everyone's taste.
○ Fresh coriander seeds are also added to the blend, which contribute both citrus notes and some of the herbal flavours typical in Gose. Goses were also originally spontaneously fermented, primarily with *Lactobacillus*, but now can be soured by a direct pitch of *Lactobacillus*, or even acidulated malt.

- Gose originates from Leipzig in Germany, first appearing in official documentation in 1332. After the reunification of Germany in 1990, Gose was granted a special dispensation from not being brewed according to the *Reinheitsgebot* as it was a regional speciality from outside Bavaria, the state that the law originally applied to. Its production had declined until it disappeared commercially in the mid-twentieth century, so its popularity now is a real success story. This renaissance is so new that, at the time of writing, *The Oxford Companion to Beer* doesn't even have an entry for it.
- Much like its other sour compatriot, Berliner Weisse, Gose can be drunk with the addition of syrup, cherry liqueur, or Echter Leipziger Allasch (a caraway liqueur) to give it a bit of sweetness and balance.
- Modern interpretations vary widely and should be approached with a touch of caution. Bayerischer Bahnhof Gose is the only authentic benchmark Gose still being produced, which gives modern producers a lot of artistic licence. Contemporary examples vary from fairly sweet and a little tart, all the way to wildly sour. Also similarly to Berliner Weisse, Goses can be found with different fruit and herb finishes.
- You should also be careful not to mistake your Gose for your Gueuze. Something that can make this a fairly challenging style to order in a noisy, busy beer bar.

**Best enjoyed:**
Go double salt and serve this as an appetiser with almonds, anchovies and olives. The coriander with shine through and the salt will get your digestive juices flowing. The distinct saltiness of Gose means you don't need much, so you can move on to something with a bit more body.

**Beers to look out for:**

○ **Unflavoured** – Bayerischer Bahnhof Gose, Westbrook Gose.

○ **Flavoured** – Westbrook Key Lime Pie Gose, Magic Rock Salty Kiss, To Øl Gose To Hollywood, Omnipollo Bianca Mango Lassi Gose, Wild Beer Co. Sleeping Lemons.

## Berliner Weisse

*See Aromatic Line, p. 53.*

**Golden Ale**

**California Common**
(Anchor Steam)

**Vienna Lager**
(Brooklyn)

**Bitter**

**Brown Ale**

**Extra Special Bitter**
(ESB)

**Old Ale**

**Dunkelweisse**

**Dubbel**

**Doppelbock**

**Quadrupel**

**Scotch Ale**

**Barley Wine**

---

 Production Method   Style

 Regional Speciality   Only open at weekends
and bank holidays

# 4. Central Line

The Central Line is the maltiest of the BeerTubeMap lines and takes you on a journey through all the levels of malt and roast. Unusually, it runs heaviest to light, left to right, starting with the blockbusters Barley Wine and Scotch Ale, through the deeply savoury dark continental beers, into the more familiar British Bitters and Browns. If you love deeper flavours, you'll love the Central Line.

## When to take the Central Line

The Central Line is the perfect line for when you're eating: the heartier your meal, the further left you should drink. It's also immensely comforting – the roasted flavours wrap you up, and give you a Ready Brek-style glow. Perfect for after a long walk when you need sustenance, which makes sense as many of the British styles on the line are stalwarts of the traditional pub.

## Stations on the Central Line

Golden Ale, California Common (Anchor Steam), Vienna Lager (Brooklyn), Bitter, Brown Ale, Extra Special Bitter (ESB), Old Ale, Dunkelweisse, Dubbel, Doppelbock, Quadrupel, Scotch Ale, Barley Wine.

## Golden Ale

*See Aromatic Line, p. 40.*

## California Common (Anchor Steam)

Anchor Steam is the best-known beer made in the California Common style, dating all the way back to the Gold Rush. German settlers used traditional techniques in a new climate, and – boom – a new style was born.

**What you need to know:**

○ California Common beers are generally very clean in character, with a slight caramel flavour. Usually dry-hopped, but with low bitterness, showcasing an earthy hop character. Even though it's made in California, the citrus and resin-heavy flavours of New World hops often associated with beers from the West Coast would not be fitting here.

○ California Common is effectively the opposite of Kölsch and Altbier: it is fermented with a lager yeast, but at warmer ale-friendly temperatures.

○ Anchor Steam is rumoured to be so-named because original brewers used wide and shallow coolships on their roofs to cool the wort (as opposed to using them for wild yeast and bacteria inoculation as in the lambic method). When transferred from the brew kettle to the coolship, the boiling hot wort would produce steam.

○ Anchor are the oldest producer of Steam Beer in California (dating back to 1896), and the most widely found, and are now the only brewery allowed to use the term 'steam' in reference to beer. This means that commercial examples are difficult to come by.

**Best enjoyed:**
As Dorothy knew, there's no place like home. So head to the home of Anchor Steam and explore San Francisco. A sprawling, hilly city where every street feels like a movie scene. It's a place to cut loose and relax, and if you get tired of the city, maybe ride a bike over the Golden Gate bridge to Sausalito, drink some Anchor and eat some Cioppino, a 'classic' Italian-American fish stew. Two things to remember: pack a jacket, the fog means it can be chilly any time of year; and never call it 'San Fran', that's for tourists, locals call it the Bay Area.

**Beers to look out for:**
Anchor Steam, Anchor Brotherhood Steam.

## Vienna Lager (Brooklyn)

Brooklyn Lager is an example of a runaway beer success and is now the main Vienna-style lager on the shelves, although Brooklyn like to say it is 'pre-Prohibition' style. Imagine drinking toasted lager: that's Vienna style.

**What you need to know:**
- ⭕ A clean and dry lager with a decidedly toasty flavour, without verging into roasty territory. It has a distinct caramel character but without any sweetness.
- ⭕ The essential difference between Vienna Lager and pale lager is the use of Vienna malt. This malt will impart the characteristic amber hue to the beer, but will also provide a lightly toasted flavour. The enzymes in Vienna malt survive the kilning process sufficiently to give it enough diastatic power (the ability to convert the starch into sugar) to be used as the entirety of the grist, without the support of any other malts, giving it a singular and unique flavour.

O Brooklyn have grown so globally successful that their lager surpasses being simply an example of the style and has now run away with and superseded the style to the point that they actually use Munich rather than Vienna malt, although to the same flavour effect.

**Best enjoyed:**
It is hard to suggest anything but in a dive bar in a Brooklyn basement, playing pool and shooting the breeze with your pals in the dim light. The Brooklyn brewery live up to their name – and embrace the East Coast NYC vibe. They label their beer as pre-Prohibition lager, but as a result of their success have become an iconic twentieth-century brand.

**Beers to look out for:**
Brooklyn Lager, Thornbridge Kill Your Darlings.

## Bitter

A traditional session ale enjoyed for its moderation in a world of crazy extremes. Usually found on cask, which gives it a smoother, easier-drinking feel.

**What you need to know:**
O Bitter is a term for an English style of ale which is low in alcohol, with a flavour that balances biscuity maltiness, apples and pears and a touch of British hops. Which means it actually isn't as bitter as its name suggests. Bitter is generally dispensed on cask, giving it a lower level of carbonation than many other beers, which makes it an easier beer to sup.

- Like some of the other stations on the BeerTubeMap, CAMRA played a big part in the transformation of Bitter. In the 1980s most beer served in pubs was pretty nondescript and came from one of a handful of big breweries. As a movement, CAMRA challenged the monopolies created by massive chains of pubs owned by breweries and inspired independents to up their game by using local small brewers. The result of these campaigns was more variety and quality in traditional beers.
- Bitters are arguably very close to pale ales, and to confuse things further brewers in the nineteenth century would label their beer for draught-dispense 'Bitter', and the same beer in bottles as 'Pale Ale'. The styles are now more distinct, as Pale Ales have a tendency to show off more hop aromatics, and are likely to use New World or American hop varieties.
- Within the Bitter category there are a few sub-categories, with minor differences in bitterness or ABV. For the purposes of this station, the best examples are those labelled as 'Ordinary Bitter', but those labelled as Special or Best Bitter also do the job. Further down the Central Line, you'll encounter ESB (see p. 61), which is significantly maltier than these examples and merits its own station.

**Best enjoyed:**
If ever there was an ode to the English pub, it would have to be this. Find one with an interesting microculture of locals and while away the afternoon pretending not to eavesdrop. The sessionability of Bitter means you can spend a few hours in the pub and still maintain use of your legs.

**Beers to look out for:**
Adnams Southwold Bitter, Fuller's Chiswick Bitter, Marble Manchester Bitter, Timothy Taylor's Landlord, Moor Revival, Swannay Orkney Best.

# Brown Ale

Brown Ale can provide incredible bang for its buck in terms of flavour, although it is a much maligned style, due to poor examples served at real ale festivals.

**What you need to know:**

O Brown Ale at its best has deep hazelnut notes and rich, tooth-cracking toffee flavours; it is the embodiment of autumn in a glass both in flavour and colour.

O This is another style where a delineation between traditional UK and US styles is made. American examples bring in an aromatic hoppy character to complement the malt, whereas UK examples focus entirely on showcasing the nutty, caramel characteristics from the malt.

O The grist for a Brown Ale will consist primarily of pale malt, with a few other varieties thrown in. Historically, brown malt would have been used, but over time developments in malting technology have brought us malts that can lend the same colour and flavour, but with more efficient sugar yields.

**Best enjoyed:**

Brown Ales are a particularly old-school style and thus are typically served on cask in the UK. As such they can most reliably be found at pubs with a strong reputation for high cellar standards. Given their rich, nutty flavours Brown Ales tend to start popping up as we move into autumn, and make a fabulous reward if you've had to walk a long way to find a decent pub in the middle of nowhere.

**Beers to look out for:**

○ **UK style:** Samuel Smith's Nut Brown Ale.
○ **US style:** Anchor Brekles Brown, Brooklyn Brown Ale, The Kernel India Brown Ale.

## Extra Special Bitter (ESB)

*See Discovery Line, p. 61.*

## Old Ale

*See Discovery Line, p. 63.*

## Dunkelweisse

Imagine being able to drink a banoffee pie, but refreshing, drinkable by the pint and without cloying sweetness.

**What you need to know:**

○ Dunkelweisse is as close as you can get to banoffee pie in a glass. Characteristic German breadiness emulates the piecrust, the familiar Weissbier yeast gives that big banana flavour, and the introduction of some darker caramel malts replicate the condensed milk caramel. And it's got some fizz too!

○ Like Doppelbock, Dunkelweisse is often produced using a decoction mash, which further adds to the naturally produced rich caramel flavours. In many ways, Dunkelweisse is an intriguing antidote to the silly syrup-filled Imperial Stouts that have started to appear. It is possible to achieve enormous depth of flavour and sweetness without cheating!

O Most Weissbier is now pale, but historically darker beers were more prevalent, due to less temperature control in the kilns during malting. This was particularly the case in the Munich area, where the local water chemistry favoured these darker malts. Whilst the rest of the world has moved on, it's great to still get these dark wheat beers on the market.

**Best enjoyed:**
Watching the game with piles of BBQ ribs and wings. German wheat beer styles are good at standing up to spice, but more in the smoky TexMex and Southern American BBQ style than the blazing heat of a vindaloo. Well worth a spin against a bitter Mexican mole, it will also beautifully accentuate the burnt and caramelised flavours found in chicken skin and BBQ burnt ends. Even better, the high carbonation of Dunkelweisse will happily cut through fatty dishes.

**Beers to look out for:**
Erdinger Dunkel, Ayinger UrWeisse, Andechser Weissbier Dunkel, Anchor Winter Wheat.

## Dubbel

Akin to Doppelbock, but this time being used by Belgian Trappist monks for sustenance. Rich, dark and full of tropical fruit flavours produced during fermentation.

**What you need to know:**

- This is the second step along the Trappist path of styles and amps up the complexity from the lesser-seen Trappist 'Single', Dubbels are full of raisiny depth that combine with fresh notes of pear, pineapple and honey and a deeper, spicier edge. This combination gives the beer a long flavour that lingers on.

- Almost all of the dried fruit flavour in Dubbel is produced by the yeast during fermentation. The malt bill of a Dubbel is generally straightforward Pilsner malt, with a bit of candi sugar to help hit the higher alcohol levels and increase the fermentability of the wort. The result is a distinct raisin flavour without a sweet finish.

- Many Belgian and Trappist ales share a distinctly ester flavour. This comes from fermenting at warmer temperatures (25–28°C) to encourage a more complete and dry fermentation, but also to promote ester formation. Esters are generally produced during fermentation by the joining of an acid molecule and an alcohol molecule to produce highly volatile aromatic compounds that can have aromas of pears, pineapple, honey and banana.

- In brewing Dubbels it is critical to balance the ester production up against production of spicy and smoky phenol flavours. Too much of one or the other would be unacceptable.

**Best enjoyed:**

Dubbel fills a particularly niche role and is best reached for when you're looking for complexity and depth, but don't feel like the roasty, coffee sweetness proffered by Imperial Stout. Try it after a meal instead of a digestif or coffee: it'll give you all the flavour without the bitterness.

**Beers to look out for:**
Westmalle Dubbel, Stringers Furness Abbey, La Trappe Dubbel, Rochefort 6, Chimay Rouge, Lost Abbey Lost and Found, Buxton Dubbel.

## Doppelbock

An old-school German style known by many as Liquid Bread and double the strength of standard beer.

**What you need to know:**

O An intense and rich beer (7% ABV) for sipping and savouring. It treads the line between sweet and savoury with a complex palate of bready caramel and dried fruit flavours and offers more than a nod to umami.

O This is a liquid ode to the Maillard reaction, the reaction between amino acids and reducing sugars. This reaction is so important in food: it gives bread its crusty flavour and appearance, is responsible for the unmistakable flavour in seared steaks, and is also the same process that gives us different flavours from different grades of malted barley. This is achieved in Doppelbocks by the weird process of decoction mashing, a complex and time-consuming mashing process where a portion of a mash is pulled off and boiled, resulting in some caramelisation and light tannin extraction, before being added back into the mash.

O The 'Liquid Bread' nickname dates back to when these beers were typically produced in German monasteries, and were lower in alcohol but higher in residual sugars, and were thus useful for nourishing the monks.

O Many Doppelbocks have goats on their labels, which is a historical play on words. In the seventeenth century a strong beer from Einbeck became popular in Munich, where the locals pronounced it 'ein Bock', which is also the word for a billy goat. The mispronunciation stuck and now Bock is the name of a strong lager across Germany.

**Best enjoyed:**
The rich umami nature of Doppelbock lends itself to a cheese board, particularly given its 7% ABV. Try it after dinner with some unctuous camembert and enjoy the way the flavours collide.

**Beers to look out for:**
Ayinger Celebrator, Paulaner Salvator, Augustiner Maximator, To Øl Mr. Brown.

## Quadrupel

The very top end of the Trappist spectrum, Quadrupel is a beer style that feels far too outlandishly decadent for a monastic life.

**What you need to know:**
O Sometimes referred to as Belgian Dark Strong Ale, Quadrupel is a darker beer than its Trappist relatives, being in excess of 9% ABV. Luscious and full of body, Quadrupels are packed full of sinfully gluttonous notes of raisins, rum, figs and a decidedly wine-like character. There will be a reasonable alcoholic burn in the mix too.
O Candi sugar is an essential ingredient to help develop those complex, dark-fruit and rum notes, but also to help hit the very high sugar content required to create the strength and mouthfeel.
O This style gained broader coverage when the highly sought-after, and very elusive Westvleteren XII was crowned the best beer in the world by Ratebeer in 2014. However, this in

itself prompted discussion around whether it was in fact the best beer, or if its rating was being bumped up by its rarity.

O The abbey at Westvleteren only produces 60,000 cases annually, but does allow you to call up its almost constantly engaged hotline and try to reserve a small quantity for collection. You have to specify exactly when you will collect, and your car licence plate. One strict condition of this process is that you absolutely must not put the bottles on sale.

**Best enjoyed:**
This is another beer where the affinity between cheese and beer gets even more magical. The fattiness of the cheese balances the higher alcohol of the beer, which in turn cuts through the fat of the cheese. And those sweeter, magical rum and raisin characteristics offset the flavours of more mature cheeses. Try it with an aged Gouda like Prima Donna for a Dutch–Belgian neighbourly pairing.

**Beers to look out for:**
St Bernardus ABT 12, Rochefort 10, Westvletern XII, Struise Pannepot, La Trappe Quadrupel, Straffe Hendrik Quadrupel, Gulden Draak 9000 Quadruple.

## Scotch Ale

A boisterously, malty heavyweight with more wanderlust than its name would suggest.

**What you need to know:**
O A close neighbour to English-style Barley Wine, Scotch Ale is a riot of flavours and texture. In the glass it is reminiscent of Scottish tablet (a less buttery form of fudge to the rest of

the us), tooth-destroying toffee and dense caramel, with a pronounced maltiness stopping it from being overly sweet. It is a lengthy boil that gives it the flavours of caramelisation, rather than the more usual wide variety of speciality malts. Although it is known as Scotch Ale, this style can be made worldwide.

O Although not historically accurate, a lot of modern versions choose to throw in a touch of peated malt, but this is arguably an Americanisation of the style. Any smoky character historically found in Scotch Ale should be attributed to phenols produced by the yeast during fermentation.

O At the beginning of the twentieth century Scotch Ales were fashionable in Belgium, and to this day some are still produced there. However, they have left a significantly larger legacy in a benchmark classic Belgian beer. Noted brewing scientist Jean de Clerck propagated the yeast from a bottled-conditioned McEwan's Scotch Ale and selected his favourite strains to create what went on to become the iconic Golden Strong Ale, Duvel (see p. 54).

**Best enjoyed:**
It makes a lot of sense to enjoy your Scotch Ale as a 'hauf and hauf' alongside a dram of Scotland's national drink. The sweetness will help it stand up to even the strongest, most pungent whisky and fight its corner up against anything particularly hot, or cask strength, even serving as a partner to old grain whisky.

**Beers to look out for:**
Alesmith Wee Heavy, Traquair House Ale, Tempest Old Parochial, Oskar Blues Old Chub, Gordon Finest Scotch.

# Barley Wine

Barley Wine is a style to be treated with serious respect, and approached with caution. As the name suggests, this is one of the styles where ABV soars and can approach that of wine.

**What you need to know:**

O  Barley Wine lives up to the wine bit of its name, with a heavy dose of raisin on the palate and an almost fortified wine taste, not least because it also has a robust sweetness. But it is most definitely beer and not wine, so this intense wine-iness is combined with some broader orange and pear flavours, all of which are balanced by a peppery bitterness from a sizeable dose of hops. It is potent stuff, generally with an ABV of 7% to 14%, another characteristic shared with wine.

O  The use of hops is what (broadly) splits Barley Wine into two categories: American and English. The essential difference is that American-style Barley Wines are typically more highly hopped, and with more intensely aromatic American varieties. Despite this, English Barley Wines can still have up to 70 IBUs, but this intense bitterness is cancelled out by the residual sweetness.

O  Barley Wine gets its unique intense flavour, colour and strength from a long boil, which further concentrates the sugar content of the wort by evaporating off the water, and also caramelises the sugars. This means there's plenty of sugar to convert to alcohol, and some left over. The caramelisation gives it its rich colour, which can range from a rich copper to a deep mahogany.

- Due to their high ABV and residual sweetness Barley Wines are brilliant cellar fodder, with many having a shelf life in the region of twenty-five years, developing more complexity and flavour as they age. It is also very common to see barrel-aged editions of Barley Wines, adding even further complexity, with a finish in whisky or wine-seasoned barrels. Unlike other strong beers like stout and porter, it is rare that other ingredients are added for flavour.
- Baladin's Xyauyù is a truly fascinating take on the aged character of Barley Wine that makes use of macro-oxidation to take the style to another level of complexity and really amp up the raisin and sherry notes typically found.

**Best enjoyed:**
It is probably irresponsible, given their high ABV, but Barley Wines can work at the end of lengthy tastings or a big meal. They add to the warm glow of a long night spent with friends seeing away a bounty of incredible beer. Usually swiftly followed by a taxi home.

**Beers to look out for:**
- **English-style** – Swannay Old Norway, De Molen Bommen & Granaten, J.W. Lee's Harvest Ale, Adnams Tally-Ho.
- **American-style** – Sierra Nevada Bigfoot, Anchor Old Foghorn, Firestone Walker Sucaba, Lost Abbey Angel's Share.

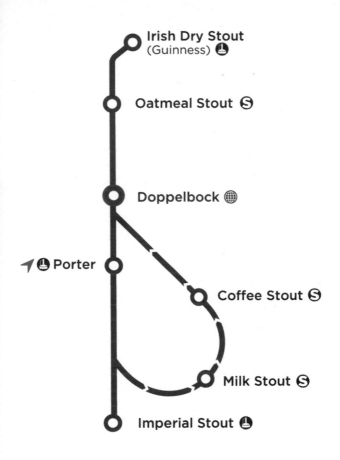

**Irish Dry Stout**
(Guinness)

**Oatmeal Stout** Ⓢ

**Doppelbock** 🌐

**Porter**

**Coffee Stout** Ⓢ

**Milk Stout** Ⓢ

**Imperial Stout**

---

🍺 Production Method      Ⓢ Style      ➤ Starting point

🌐 Regional Speciality

# 5. Indulgence Line

Also known as the dark side. Don't let the darkness of these beers put you off; they are roasted, rich, deep and chocolatey and could easily replace a meal or dessert – depending on the sweetness of your tooth. The stations on the line consist of porters and stouts, with various additions to tweak the flavours. As you travel around the loop at the southern end you'll find more sweetness and a lighter style at the northern tip. Of all the lines, the Indulgence Line stations are most similar, meaning if you enjoy one you're likely to enjoy most of them.

## When to take the Indulgence Line
When you need something filling and delicious, or instead of a nightcap at the end of the night. If you need a bit of a treat, dig into a bar of chocolate or chocolate brownie and one of these ... ultimate luxury.

Indulgence Line beers are also great options for people who don't yet love beer, but do love coffee and chocolate.

## Stations on the Indulgence Line
Irish Dry Stout (Guinness), Oatmeal Stout, Doppelbock, Porter, Imperial Stout, Milk Stout, Coffee Stout.

## Irish Dry Stout (Guinness)

Despite being quite an acquired taste this is one of the world's most widely consumed styles, albeit most of it from a single brand. A pint of the black stuff is a firm favourite from Dublin to Durban.

**What you need to know:**

O Although imposingly midnight black in colour, Irish Dry Stout is an ultimately sessionable drink, with an ABV around 4%, which – unlike some other stout varieties – finishes nice and dry. It combines bitter, roasted flavours with a hint of dark fruits and just a nod to malty caramel.

O The rise of Irish stout in the nineteenth century can be partially attributed to a tax loophole. At the time tax was paid on ingredients, specifically malt and hops, not on alcohol like today. Arthur Guinness had the idea to use a proportion of roasted unmalted barley in the grist to get around this. It is this roasted barley that gives the beer its distinctive colour and bitter coffee-like flavour.

O A key feature of Irish Dry Stout, especially Guinness, is the use of nitrogen for the dispense gas. Although nitrogen can inhibit expression of flavour and aroma in beer, it gives an incredibly creamy and dense mouthfeel, due to the fact that the bubbles are significantly smaller than those produced by carbon dioxide.

**Best enjoyed:**

In Galway, a pretty city on the west coast of Ireland. It's a feast for your eyes, belly, ears and soul! By day wander the lanes, admire the colourful painted houses or gaze out at Galway Bay. By night there are plenty of pubs and bars, full of music and banter. And don't miss out on the plentiful Atlantic seafood brought in by the local fishing boats. Whether you like it white tablecloth or from a market stall, you'll find something for your Guinness to wash down.

**Beers to look out for:**
Guinness, The Kernel Dry Stout, Buxton Rednik, Murphy's Irish Stout.

## Oatmeal Stout

A revival stout variety, where the magic of oats adds a luxurious creamy quality to the rich, dark flavours of stout.

### What you need to know:
O Oatmeal Stout is rich in texture and flavour but not overpowering. It has a voluptuous creamy texture and medium body, and is likely to have a combination of toffee, malted milk, chocolate and espresso flavours. It is slightly sweeter than traditional stouts and often has less roast and bitterness. The hop level can differ from brewer to brewer but there should not be prominent hop aromas.
O Oatmeal Stout uses a proportion of oatmeal (cooked and pressed oats) in the mash. This addition is more to do with texture than flavour: the extra protein found in oats makes the final beer taste smoother and creamier, and makes the head last longer too. They also release a small amount of unfermented sugars, which adds to the creamy sensation.
O Oatmeal Stout is another beer with traditional roots which is enjoying a very modern revival. Oats would have been part of the grains used to make beer in northern and Scottish communities as part of the local crop, but this was gradually moved away as brewers sought consistency in their beers. Oatmeal Stout was popular in the mid twentieth century but died out again in the 1970s. The most recent

revival has taken seed on both sides of the Atlantic, and is part of a popular wave of fuller styles of beer and gourmand flavours.

**Best enjoyed:**
Follow a (tenuous) Scottish oaty link and head to Edinburgh, a hub for brewing, breweries and beer drinking. The compact nature of Scotland's capital means you can explore most of the nooks and crannies on foot, from the traditional wood-panelled Scottish bars to up-to-the-minute craft bars with micro-breweries and 400-bottle lists. All this in the shadow of a medieval castle and an extinct volcano to climb to blow away those cobwebs.

**Beers to look out for:**
Fourpure Oatmeal Stout, Tiny Rebel Dirty Stop Out, Black Isle Hibernator, Vocation Cloak and Dagger.

## Doppelbock

*See Central Line, p. 84.*

## Porter

A dark, rich and chocolatey ale that is neither too acrid nor too heavy – but beware, the world of porter, stout, American- or English-style is a complex one!

**What you need to know:**
O A smooth, relatively easy-drinking dark ale that is deceptively light on the palate given its intense, rich,

chocolate and coffee flavours. It can range in colour from chocolate-brown to near-black, but while every brewer's Porter will differ, you should always get a hint of sweetness in your glass.

O Porter's rich and dark flavours come solely from heavy roasting of a variety of malts. There is no set recipe, so brewers can play with the ratios of different types of malt used and how much they are roasted. However, around 95 per cent of a Porter's recipe is usually pale malt.

O What we currently know as Porter bears very little relation to its anecdotal origin. Allegedly, in the eighteenth century, porter was a cheaper blend of a number of different casks (sometimes used to mask stale or spoiled beer), which was then built into a recipe replicating this flavour, which became instantly popular among dock-workers, or porters. Porter Stout was a stronger version of Porter, although this differentiation no longer stands true.

O American-style Porters generally have a slightly higher ABV and be more heavily hopped, and fuller in body, than the English styles.

**Best enjoyed:**
Typically considered a winter beer style, but why not up-end this and knock yourself up a Porter affogato in the height of summer by adding a measure of Porter to a scoop of ice cream? A generous scoop of classic vanilla ice cream is the obvious choice, but don't be afraid to play with the wide flavours found in Porter, like coffee, hazelnut or chocolate.

**Beers to look out for:**
Anchor Porter, The Kernel Export India Porter, Fuller's London Porter, Brew By Numbers 03/ (various editions), Traditional Porter, Five Points Railway Porter.

# Imperial Stout

Big, punchy, strong and dark. Imperial Stout can be widely interpreted to show off the whole spectrum of malt flavours from dry and ultra-roasty to super-sweet, as well as adding extra flavours.

**What you need to know:**

O The mark of a quality Imperial Stout is ultimately a dark beer with roasted chocolate and malt flavours that has a lofty ABV without coming across as overly hot and boozy-tasting or acrid. However, it's difficult to nail down the exact flavour of Imperial Stout as there have been a number of trends that have pulled the flavour profile in many directions. There was a race to develop stouts as strong as humanly possible, then a barrel-aging revolution brought immense oak notes and spirit finishes; finally the public's sweet tooth kicked in and chocolate syrup and vanilla came to the fore of the desired flavours. Now Imperial Stout is at a point where if you can think of a barrel type, or a loosely dessert-related adjunct, it's probably happened.

O Similar to IPA, Imperial Stout was primarily a British export product, in this case being favoured by blue-blooded Russians. Napoleon's invasion of Russia and economic isolation of Britain cut off the supply route, but brewers still produced the style and it became increasingly popular in the UK.

O Although Imperial Stouts are generally not full of hop flavours, they are high in IBUs, typically with levels around 80. This is to balance the sweetness of the extremely high gravity wort required to create the body and alcohol, and produce a well-rounded final beer.

O Many smaller breweries use a double mash to achieve the high gravity wort needed to ferment to such a high ABV. This means the brewer doesn't have to rely on an extremely long boil to concentrate the wort to a higher gravity, and can thus build the desired colour into their mash recipe.

**Best enjoyed:**
An Imperial Stout makes for an incredible midnight feast. Roasty and bitter examples play beautifully with complex stinky cheeses and cured meats. Alternatively, go to the other end of the spectrum and use it as a replacement in the classic milk-and-cookies combo. Or enjoy your barrel-aged stout with its spirit sibling as a twist on a hauf and a hauf (the Scottish half-pint and whisky chaser).

**Beers to look out for:**
O **Unflavoured** – Swannay Orkney Porter, North Coast Old Rasputin, Samuel Smith's Imperial Stout, Evil Twin Even More Jesus.
O **Flavoured (adjunct)** – Founder's KBS, Buxton/Omnipollo Yellow Belly, Mikkeller Beer Geek Dessert Edition, Wild Beer Co. Wildebeest.
O **Flavoured (barrel)** – Goose Island Bourbon County, Deschutes the Abyss, Old Chimneys Good King Henry Special Reserve.

## Milk Stout

One of the few beer styles, or even fermented drinks, that will easily please anybody craving the sugary side of things. This is a beer equivalent of a latte or mocha. Although there is a little cheating involved.

**What you need to know:**

O Milk Stout is a sweet style of stout that combines the distinctive roasty, coffee and bitter chocolate flavours of stout with a dairy character and sense of creaminess created by more sweetness and body.

O Unfortunately for vegans, Milk Stouts are brewed with the addition in the boil of lactose, the sugar most commonly found in milk. Most strains of brewer's yeast can't break down this sugar, formed of a galactose molecule joined to a glucose molecule. Like the unfermentable dextrins formed during a mash, lactose will stick about after fermentation and give the beer added body and a perceivable sweetness.

O During the early twentieth century this type of beer was marketed to pregnant women and runners for its supposed health benefits, and was generally quite low in ABV. However, there is currently a growing trend for using lactose to make super-sweet, high-ABV 'adjunct' stouts, that taste of cupcakes, ice cream and other things for those of a sweet tooth. Not so healthy ...

**Best enjoyed:**
Only if you have a very sweet tooth! These are definitely instead of, not as well as, the dessert option. But they can be a great alternative to a hot chocolate at the end of the night or if you're warming up after you've been out in the cold.

**Beers to look out for:**
- **Unflavoured** – BBF Milk Stout, Left Hand Milk Stout, Wiper and True Milkshake, Galway Bay Buried at Sea, To Øl By Udder Means.
- **Flavoured** – Stone Xocoveza, Wild Beer Co. Millionaire, Fallen Chew Chew, Omnipollo Noa Pecan Mud, Pilot Mochaccino.

## Coffee Stout

Coffee and stout are both experiencing revolutions, so it's not a surprise there has been a crossover point, and it's here at Coffee Stout.

**What you need to know:**

O Of course, Coffee Stout tastes of coffee, but it's a bittersweet pairing of coffee with a deep maltiness and hints of chocolate, dark fruits and caramel. Expect richness in every sense, with a relatively high ABV and full texture. The bitterness of the coffee does enough to balance any chocolatey sweetness to create something that is far greater than the sum of its parts.

O The parallels between coffee and beer are very clear. Coffee geeks talk about single origin beans and new and exciting brewing methods, and there's a deep focus on flavour. Stout has presented itself as the easiest and most logical point for coffee to segue with beer, given the common flavour profiles of the two.

O At its most simple level Coffee Stout does involve adding coffee to stout, but you can't just tip beans into the mix. Added too early in the fermentation, a lot of the more delicate flavours of coffee can be pulled away by the carbon dioxide produced, and it ends up tasting like chilli.

O Brewers have now begun to embrace one of the on-trend techniques of 'craft coffee', and have started blending their stouts with cold-brew coffee. This is where ground coffee beans are left in cold water for a period of around twenty-four hours to extract the flavour. The cold-brew technique produces an extract stronger in flavour than the usual hot method, but significantly less acidic and a touch sweeter, making it the perfect partner to a big stout.

**Best enjoyed:**

As a thoroughly luxurious and alternative approach to meeting a friend for a coffee. Pair it up with a stupidly gooey brownie, preferably made with the same beer as a key ingredient. Just use a splash in the brownie mix and use the rest of the bottle to reward yourself after doing the washing-up.

**Beers to look out for:**

Arbor Breakfast Stout, Mikkeller Beer Geek Breakfast, Buxton Extra Porter, Siren Broken Dreams, Pilot Mochaccino, Alesmith Speedway Stout.

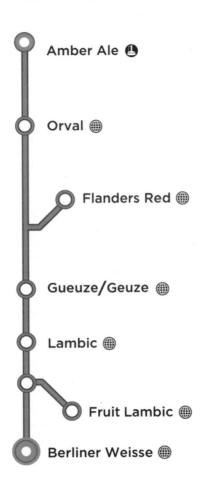

Amber Ale

Orval

Flanders Red

Gueuze/Geuze

Lambic

Fruit Lambic

Berliner Weisse

---

 Production Method

 Regional Speciality

# 6. Epicurean Line

You could argue that this is the best line on the BeerTubeMap because it takes you somewhere you didn't even know existed and would never have set out for. Beers on the Epicurean Line are unique and challenging, encompassing sour, savoury and 'funk'– a bona fide, if slightly nebulous, beer term referring to the wild, earthy and unconventional flavours which have become very popular in some craft beer circles; tasting notes include horse sweat, germolene and farmyard! The flavours might seem unusual for beer but they go back to very traditional beer-making. The beers are made using wild yeasts or bacteria, some even welcome flavours of oxidation and are often aged, all of which add to their complex flavours. They may sound odd, but once you've visited you may fall in love with their wild ways.

**When to take the Epicurean Line**

When you are feeling bold! Epicurean Line beers should be sampled before you buy, so a bar or pub with a varied list is a good starting point, and you should give yourself a bit of time with them to get used to the flavours.

Epicurean stations also work beautifully with artisan cheeses that have been made with raw milk – they share some of that funky flavour.

**Stations on the Epicurean Line**

Amber Ale, Orval, Flanders Red, Gueuze, Lambic, Fruit Lambic, Berliner Weisse.

## Amber Ale

*See Discovery Line, p. 65.*

## Orval

A unique monastic speciality praised by beer lovers globally.

**What you need to know:**

○ Orval is a deep amber colour, and pleasantly bitter with a touch of residual sweetness. Depending on its age there should be a tropical note on the nose and a distinct hop character.

○ The Orval brewery is unusual because, unlike other Trappist breweries, they only produce one beer commercially, Orval, although they do make the Petite Orval purely for consumption by the monks and visitors to the local café. It doesn't fit neatly with any of the other Trappist beer styles – Dubbel, Tripel or Quadrupel – having its own unique style.

○ Orval's use of *Brettanomyces* (Brett) in bottling is what sets it entirely apart from any others. This 'wild' yeast strain will happily tick away over the years feeding on complex sugars that traditional brewer's yeast can't consume, drying the beer out and adding more carbonation. During this time the hop character of the beer begins to fade, and some of the more interesting flavours produced by Brett take hold, such as pineapple and coconut. As such the beer tastes completely different when it is fresh compared to when it is aged. Many bars and shops build historic stocks in order to hold vertical tastings and compare these differences.

○ This beer has historically been dry-hopped for additional aroma since the 1930s, a technique only rediscovered by American 'craft' brewers in the 1970s.

**Best enjoyed:**
Consensus seems to suggest that Orval strikes its prime at around eighteen months old, but equally it is a delight fresh. One of the best places to find out for yourself is North Bar in Leeds, where they regularly have stock of Orval of a few different 'vintages'. Take your time over a bottle of each and really dig into the nuances of each different 'vintage'. However, it should be noted that oldest doesn't automatically mean best: even when stored in perfect conditions, after a certain point flavours of oxidation start to become evident.

**Beers to look out for:**
Orval.

# Flanders Red

A truly fascinating confluence of beer, wine and even balsamic vinegar, in terms both of production methods and flavour profile. This Flemish regional delicacy is a wild ride.

**What you need to know:**

○ Flanders Red is an incredibly complex style full of dark fruit and tea flavours, tannins, savoury, deep oak character, and at times a lick of wicked balsamic vinegar acidity. There are no shortcuts with this style, the wort is fermented in oak vats, or foeders, with a normal yeast strain, but the *Acetobacter*, *Lactobacillus* and *Brettanomyces* cultures resident in the oak also contribute to the intensely multifaceted flavour.

○ To achieve balance, Flanders Reds are often blends of beers of different ages, with older beer contributing more acidity and oak character, and younger beers bringing a residual sweetness to round things out.

○ Although an acetic element is to be expected, your Flanders Red should not taste like vinegar. This element should really be part of the broader spectrum that builds this beer, rather than stealing the show itself.

**Best enjoyed:**
Given its similarity to Burgundy wine, this is a tremendous style for pairing with food and creating some innovative pairings. It will play nicely with dark chocolate and big meaty flavours. A strongly recommended pairing that plays on the balsamic aspect is with a very simple plate of fresh strawberries garnished with cracked black pepper.

**Beers to look out for:**

- **Traditional** – Rodenbach Grand Cru, Rodenbach Vintage, Duchesse de Bourgogne, Vichtenaar, Bruery Terreux Oude Tart.
- **Flavoured** – Rodenbach Caractère Rouge, Lost Abbey Red Poppy, Cascade Sang Royal, Thornbridge Love Among the Ruins.

## Gueuze/Geuze

Often referred to as 'the champagne of beer', but it could be argued that champagne was the Gueuze of wine. Gueuze blends different vintages of spontaneously fermented lambic to create a complex and delicious beer.

**What you need to know:**

- Gueuze is a funky, sour blend capable of displaying a wide variety of flavours and aromas. One of the most peculiar tasting notes found in beer is the 'aroma of horse blanket', and arguably Gueuze is the prime example of this. It has a musty, earthy, farmyard note that combines the smell of saddles and horse sweat with that of baked fruit and nuts. This, when balanced against delicate acidity and effervescence, amounts to a beautiful experience.
- The spelling of Gueuze can differ depending on the area of the Pajottenland it is produced in; French-speakers tend to use the Gueuze spelling whereas the Flemish spelling is Geuze.
- Like many whiskies and wines, it can elicit a spiritual response from beer lovers, who often describe it as the result of a confluence of art, science and faith because of the complex production which, unlike many beers produced commercially, relies on nature and time.

- Old lambic (typically three years old) that still contains live but dormant yeast and bacteria, is blended with young lambic (usually one year old, but quite often some two years old) that still contains fermentable sugars. This blend will then naturally re-ferment in the bottle, producing bubbles and a yeast sediment that requires the bottles to be served from a basket in order to keep the yeast from ending up in the glass.
- Some producers will release special editions that also contain lambic as old as four years old. The lambic at this age starts to show the pronounced notes of nutty oxidation, given its longer time in the barrels.
- One of the curious things about Gueuze is that many of the producers will not physically brew anything themselves. They buy in wort from other brewers and rack it to ferment in barrels in their own warehouses, which they can then build their own blends from.
- Although Gueuze tastes exceptional when it is fresh, it can benefit from additional periods of ageing. This has led to a trend of people visiting producers and buying as much stock as they can, and then hoarding the bottles for multiple years.

**Best enjoyed:**
One of the best places to experience Gueuze is at the Brussels Gueuze Museum, AKA Brasserie Cantillon. Here you can take a self-guided tour of one of the world's best producers, wander through their vast barrel stores, and admire the spiders that carefully guard the fermenting barrels from flies and other creatures. Once finished, take a seat in the bar area and work your way through an incredible list of rarities for consumption on-site only. In terms of true Gueuze culture, make a pilgrimage out to 'In de Verzekering tegen de Grote Dorst' (In the Insurance Against Great Thirst) half an hour's drive from Brussels, and strictly only open on a Sunday just in time for the

end of mass. Here you'll see the old parishioners start their Sunday off with a lovely glass of Gueuze.

**Beers to look out for:**
Boon Geuze, Cantillon Gueuze, 3 Fonteinen Oude Geuze, De Cam Oude Geuze, Hanssens Oude Gueuze, Gueuze Lindemans Cuvée René, Timmermans Oude Gueuze, Tilquin Oude Gueuze.

## Lambic

The curious and unique speciality of the Belgian province of Pajottenland, impossible to reproduce anywhere else in the world.

**What you need to know:**

○ Most Lambic produced is used to build blends for Gueuze or Fruit Lambics, but once aged can also be served on its own. Depending on its age, Lambic can express a wide variety of aromas and flavours, from savoury and nutty 'cellar' aromas and cheesiness, all the way to ripe orchard fruit and a vinous, grapey flavour. Lambic should be sour, but crucially not have an overly acetic vinegar character. It is usually dispensed from ceramic jugs or bag in boxes. Straight Lambic is flat or has very subtle natural carbonation.

○ Lambic is an unblended, spontaneously fermented, complex sour beer with layers of unusual and varied flavours. These come from the production process, which is unconventional when compared to other brewing processes, leaving a lot of steps to naturally occur. Lambic must be made from a mash containing at least 30 per cent unmalted wheat, using an extremely complex mash regime known as turbid mashing, that to other brewers would appear counter-intuitive, as the aim is to produce a cloudy and starchy wort. Continuing this contrariness, the wort is then boiled with extremely pungent cheesy hops that are a few years old. After the boil the wort is pumped into the koelschip (coolship), a wide and shallow vessel, and left to cool overnight. The vats are left open so the air passing over them can inoculate the beer with the wild yeasts and bacteria unique to the Pajottenland. Once inoculated and cooled it is transferred to ferment in unbunged oak barrels, or foeders. These wild yeasts and bacteria mean the beer is unique to the area and unreplicable.

○ Lambic can sometimes be served as a Faro, where a sweeter 'non-lambic' beer, or candi sugar, is blended into the Lambic at the bar, to balance the sourness. These are traditionally not bottled because the blend of the sugar syrup and the dormant yeast in the Lambic would cause the bottle to explode unless pasteurised.

○ Lambic has 'Traditional Speciality Guaranteed' status from the EU, which defines the geographical origin and techniques that must be adhered to, in order to be able to use the Lambic terminology.

**Best enjoyed:**
A trip out to Gooik, only half an hour from Brussels, will give you a couple of tremendous Lambic experiences only metres away from each other. Head out on a Sunday and enjoy a traditional Belgian lunch over a few glasses of Lambic at the Volkscafé De Cam. If you've timed your visit perfectly, you can head across the courtyard to Gueuzestekerij De Cam. Karel, the owner-operator, and arguably hardest-working person in beer, will happily pour you a glass and show you around his Gueuzestekerij/Blendery, where there is an opportunity to pick up some of his straight Lambic in bottles, or incredible Fruit Lambics and Gueuzes.

**Beers to look out for:**
Cantillon Grand Cru Bruocsella, De Cam Oude Lambiek, Timmermans Jonge Lambiek, Girardin Oude Lambik.

## Fruit Lambic

This is a style that is growing fairly rapidly, particularly through independent Lambic blenders. It spans a wide range of flavours, from syrupy sweetened stuff all the way up to extremely refined and heavily sought-after rare bottlings.

**What you need to know:**

○ Lambic beers (see p. 110) use wild yeasts to ferment the beer, giving them a sour, funky taste; imagine the difference between normal bread and sourdough – it's a similar thing. Fruit Lambics introduce a tart but sweet element by adding whole fruit or fruit juice into the young Lambic mix. The combination is a delicious mix of fruit and savoury character with enough funk to keep it interesting.

○ Fruit Lambics are the most widely available style of Lambic, with the most prevalent styles being Kriek and Framboise, made with cherries and raspberries respectively. This is most likely a nod to the farmhouse tradition of Lambic, and the abundance of these fruits in Belgium. For Fruit Lambics produced solely by macerating whole fruits in Lambic rather than juice, the ratio can be as high as 400 grams of fruit per litre of Lambic.

○ Blenders such as Tilquin and De Cam have begun producing small batches of Lambics flavoured with more unusual fruits, such as plums, redcurrants and blueberries among many others. Bottles of some of these small-batch Fruit Lambics can reach prices in the thousands of dollars on illicit beer-trading websites.

○ Every year since 2008 Cantillon release their 'Zwanze' (a Brussels dialect word meaning to mess around) beer. These are experimental, fun one-off editions and usually involve fruit or herbs of some description. They are released simultaneously at specially chosen locations around the world, and bottles are only available for consumption on-site at the brewery.

**Best enjoyed:**
Every two years in May the Lambic producers of the Pajottenland throw open their doors to welcome visitors for the Toer de Gueuze, many of whom never allow tours or visits. It is possible to cycle between all of the producers, or book yourself onto one of the tours organised by the HORAL committee (a producers' organisation). This is a very special occasion and many of the producers will put together one-off special editions, or pull out vintage bottles to celebrate.

**Beers to look out for:**
Cantillon Kriek, 3 Fonteinen Hommage, Tilquin Quetsche, De Cam Bosbessen, Hanssens Oudbeitje, Timmermans Oude Kriek, Boon Framboise.

## Berliner Weisse

*See Aromatic Line, p. 53.*

Helles Lager

Pilsner

Märzen

Kölsch

Premium European Lager

Altbier

Golden Ale

Extra Special Bitter (ESB)

Blonde Ale

American Pale Ale

Old Ale

Red Ale

American IPA

Amber Ale

British IPA

 Production Method

 Style

Starting point

  Regional Speciality

# 7. Explorer Loop

The Explorer Loop is the handy all-rounder line that you can hop on and off without even thinking about it. It takes in a combination of lagers, pale ales and lighter ales with a varying degree of hops and malt across them. The stations on it are all on another line on the map as well, but the loop allows you to switch across classic easy-drinking flavours with ease and grace.

**When to take the Explorer Loop**
When you fancy a selection of beers that aren't taxing but are delicious. You could easily cruise the Explorer Line all evening without tiring of the flavours. They are mostly easy to find too, so you won't be stuck in a bar without a next step available.

These beers are thirst-quenching, don't have extreme flavours and generally have a level of carbonation which makes them excellent fodder for sharing plates, charcuterie and tapas boards.

**Stations on the Explorer Loop**
Kölsch (p. 27), Golden Ale (p. 40), Blonde Ale (p. 41), American Pale Ale (p. 43), American IPA (p. 45), British IPA (p. 67), Amber Ale (p. 65), Red Ale (p. 64), Old Ale (p. 63), Extra Special Bitter (ESB) (p. 61), Altbier (p. 60), Märzen (p. 33), Pilsner (p. 32), Premium European Lager (p. 31), Helles Lager (p. 28).

# How and where to buy beer

The UK is blessed with a widespread and vibrant beer culture. Every decent-sized town will have at least one pub or bottle shop with a wide and constantly changing selection of homegrown and imported beers, and even supermarkets are waking up to the fact that consumers want an interesting selection of beer beyond the big lager names.

## STAYING IN

A well-stocked fridge at home is a beautiful thing, and there is no excuse with so many shops, websites and subscription services sourcing and selling good beers. Here's the low-down on where to buy and what you should get.

### Independent bottle shops

Our thriving culture of independent bottle shops has been one of the main driving forces behind the spread of excellent and diverse beer in the UK. With no fixed menu, it's easy for shops to get a case of something in, and then once that's sold give the shelf space to an entirely different beer. But this makes it hard to keep up, and it's easy to fall in love with something only to find it's never to return again! The answer is to make friends with your local indie and let them know when you have enjoyed something, that way they can tip you off when there's something else coming in that you'd like.

If you're looking to keep up to date it is also worth following your local independent on Twitter, as many of them post info on new products from every delivery drop they get. Even better than this, many of them will take reservations for stock over Twitter, making it easier for dedicated followers to nab rarities before they hit shelves. Most independents will also offer frequent tastings, some of which will be hosted by people from the brewery or a local distributor. These are a great opportunity to try before you buy, and get even more info and recommendations.

Many shops are starting to get behind the 'cold chain' philosophy that some modern breweries maintain, and are beginning to convert to having all of their shelf space refrigerated, which means your beers will be in even better condition when you buy them.

**Growler shops**
A very American invention, now starting to pop up in the UK, that allows you to effectively have draught beer at home. A growler is a re-sealable, airtight vessel, usually made of glass or stainless steel. These can be used to take beer dispensed on tap home, whilst retaining its condition, so it can be enjoyed within a day or two. Filling growlers is not as simple as pouring beer into any old bottle and resealing. A good growler shop will be suitably equipped to sanitise your growler, and will purge it with carbon dioxide before filling, as well as putting the cap on whilst there is a head of foam to minimise oxidation. Most growler shops will sell by the litre or multiples thereof, so make sure you get a sample before committing.

**Supermarkets**
Historically, supermarkets have always been about ultra-low-price deals on cases of industrially brewed bland lagers. Lately most of the large national supermarket chains have woken up to the enormous potential of a well-considered beer range. As well as classic UK regional breweries, they stock a handful of modern 'craft breweries' and even a number of benchmark European imports too. Many supermarkets also source local

beers from breweries within a certain radius of the stores. This is all great news, and generally these are priced in a way that makes them affordable, so if they sell your favourite they're a good place to stock up. However, if you're looking to explore and want some advice, you're unlikely to get it in a supermarket, unless you chance upon a local expert. However, in the main, the experience is completely different from shopping in an independent.

### Websites

Not everybody is fortunate enough to live or work within easy distance of a fantastic bar or shop, or have the time to peruse the shelves and make a selection. To help with this, there are now a wide variety of webshops with enormous selections that will often do next day delivery. There are even a couple of websites based in the larger cities in the UK that will deliver chilled beers to your door within a couple of hours. Some webshops get exclusive access to extremely limited specials, and you have to be quick off the mark to nail them down. Keep an eye on their social media streams and the webpage itself, and have your credit card at the ready, as those with the fastest fingers will grab the prize.

There are now a handful of breweries opening their own webshops that will allow you to pick and mix individual cans or bottles from their range, rather than full cases. These are usually used by breweries that will have multiple new releases each week, often exclusively through their webshop.

### Subscription services

There are a number of subscription services that curate a case of beer for you on a regular basis. These are especially good as a gift or if you're new to beer because they take the choice away from you and put beers in front of you that you might never try, although they can become a little repetitive after a while. The best ones have a good variety of beers and base your selection on your feedback, so you don't end up with a shelf of beers you don't like, so it's worth doing a bit of research before you commit.

## GOING OUT

One of the major barriers to beer selections in the bar and pub trade has been the 'tied' house system, where multinational brewing corporations and pub chains controlled which beers the landlords had on draught. However, the tide is finally turning and there is a resurgence in landlords who are demanding more freedom over their draught beer ranges. The result is a growing number of places opening now, completely free from tie and dedicated to a constantly rotating line-up of beer from independent brewers.

### Traditional pubs

The traditional pub is the bedrock of UK society, and one of the most evocative images of our culture, although sadly they are dying out, with pubs closing every day. Ancient wood panelling, leather seats and an open fire crackling away are the perfect partner to pints of cask ale and the chatter of a community. Although the very best of these will be focused on immaculately presented cask beer, there should also be a range of keg lager, with many now serving keg beers from local breweries. If you know a good one, look after it.

### Modern craft bars

Different from a traditional pub in look and feel, a craft bar will usually have in excess of ten different draught beers available and will offer smaller pours all the way down to a third of a pint, to allow you to try more beers in a session without getting too carried away. It is quite common to see modern 'craft' bars do away with the traditional pump clips or keg badges, in favour of a plain blackboard with the names on instead. If you need a bit more information than is on display, open up and ask your bartender – most of them are desperate to chat beer with friendly customers. These are great opportunities to roam around and it's easy to try a few different beers over the course of the evening. Most modern bars will also allow you to taste a little splash of something on draught, but be careful not to take this too far and end up asking for twenty sample pours on a busy Friday night; there will be a limit. So try two or three, pick your favourite and then try some different ones on the next round. Ultimately, if you don't take advantage of the bartender's specialist knowledge, or ask for a sample, you've only yourself to blame if you end up with a full pint of something not to your taste!

### Restaurants

Unfortunately, restaurants still lag behind when it comes to beer selection. You can enjoy an exquisite multiple course tasting menu at a Michelin star restaurant in the UK and pay well over the odds for industrially brewed, low-quality beer. Beer can enhance a dish, add extra elements and inspire the eater. It has arguably more savoury, umami elements than many wines, making it an equal alternative in matching drinks with dishes, Yet culturally it isn't considered as 'fine' as wine.

The enviable role of beer sommelier isn't a common sight in UK restaurants. However, some restaurants, generally in collaboration with a producer or supplier, will run one-off beer-matched dinners, which, when done well, are worth exploring. If the chef has created his menu with the beer in mind you will find a delicious dance between glass and plate, with pairings being sometimes complementary or contrasting.

However, poor beer selections in restaurants are often due to many opening in tied units that have no say over their range. And even those with the most worthwhile intentions, pursuing a sustainable menu, end up selecting beers brewed as close as possible to them, geographically, rather than the best quality options. Ultimately, restaurants are simply more expensive than

bars or shops to run, and thus need to make higher profit margins on drinks, which often means they have to select cheaper beers that will end up on the menu at a perceived reasonable price.

This just makes a restaurant with an excellent beer offering even more special. When you find one, sing about it. Tell all of your friends, and demand a similar standard from other restaurants that you visit. The worst thing that could happen is that somebody bucks up their ideas and we end up with an even richer beer- and food-matching community.

## DISPENSE METHODS

Once upon a time beer was served from a cask and that was it. Then came bottles, kegs, cans and growlers. The dispense can be decided by the style of beer, tradition, convenience or what's currently on trend. You often don't get a choice of which dispense method your beer comes in, but it will tell you something about the style or the brewer who is making it.

### Bottle

The most commonly seen packaging method for beer, and it has been around for centuries. Bottling can be broken down further into bottle-conditioned and force-carbonated. Bottle-conditioned beer is packaged to referment and naturally carbonate in the bottle, either with a little dose of sugar, or yeast to eat up some remaining fermentable sugar, or both. With bottle-conditioned beers it is generally recommended to pour carefully to keep the yeast sediment in the bottle, although a bit of yeast won't do you any harm. The alternative is that the beer is carbonated in-tank before packaging.

Not all bottling is equal either. Clear glass bottles are an absolute no-no as these allow the beer to come into contact with UV rays which will cause skunking, a deeply unpleasant off flavour which will produce a nasty musty aroma like a skunk's spray.

Bottle beers can be particularly good for ageing, dependent on style, and providing that the seal doesn't fail. If you're looking to age a bottle, keep it in a cool, dark, dry, place with a stable temperature. With crown-cap bottles these should be kept upright, but bottles packaged with a cork and cage (champagne style) can be aged horizontally.

**Can**

Canned beer is undergoing an unbelievable renaissance. Once prohibitively expensive and only available to massive breweries, canning line manufacturers have made advances to bring pricing within the reach of small independent brewers. Unlike bottles, cans offer up 100 per cent of their surface area as a blank canvas for the incredible branding favoured by the modern craft scene, and many of them end up looking too pretty to drink.

Historically, cans have been perceived as an inferior method of packaging, as they were generally used for mass-produced, flavourless lager. A common criticism was that when drinking from the can these beers would taste tinny or metallic. Drinking straight from the can (or bottle), is the equivalent to looking at a massive painting through a tiny keyhole. Pour it into a glass, and get the full value of the incredible aroma and appearance of the beer.

Cans don't allow any UV access to the beer, so there should be absolutely no skunking. Additionally, they are significantly lighter in weight than bottles, and when packaged into boxes waste very little space, thus they are much more environmentally friendly to ship.

However, there is a downside. Some brewers end up buying the cheapest canning line possible, or use questionable mobile canning lines, purely to take advantage of the trend for canned beers. This can result in poorly seamed cans, with lots of oxygen in the final product, making it spoil quickly.

## Cask

The most traditional dispense method, but almost totally unique to the UK. Live beer is delivered to the pub cellar and still needs to undergo a secondary fermentation. Because of this finishing process in the pub, cask beer needs care and attention from trained staff to be dispensed properly. This dependency on the pub to ensure the final quality of the beer has caused some modern breweries to pull out of cask production, as some pubs don't give proper training or time to finish the beer properly.

Cask beer is dispensed without the use of extraneous carbon dioxide, and at the ambient temperature of the pub cellar. The beer is pumped from the cellar by using a 'beer engine', which pulls a slight vacuum on the cask and thus pulls the beer up through the line. Occasionally electric pumps can be used.

Well looked after cask beer is an incredibly rewarding drink, for both the customer and the landlord.

## Keg

Keg is the preferred dispense method of most modern breweries. This is where the beer is dispensed, already carbonated, from a pressurised container, and passed through a chiller to bring it down to only a few degrees centigrade. Keg became popular as the already finished beer is allowed little opportunity for error once delivered to a bar cellar. This is not to say that keg is simply 'plug and play'; it still requires the bar to take care of the beer.

CAMRA typically opposes keg beer as it is normally pasteurised and force-carbonated, or served in a method where the beer comes into contact with carbon dioxide gas. However, some beers are keg-conditioned and carbonated naturally with a final secondary fermentation in the keg so no extraneous carbon dioxide is used. And innovations like KeyKeg are overcoming these barriers in order to meet CAMRA's requirements. Expect to see more innovations in this field.

## MATCHING/PAIRING

Beer is often overlooked when it comes to matching food and drink, in deference to its swankier cousin, wine. Even though it could be argued beer has just as much, if not more, to bring to the table when served with the right dish.

One of the main differences between wine and beer is the carbonation in beer: the bubbles in the beer cleanse your mouth of any traces of fat or oiliness from the food, leaving your mouth refreshed after every mouthful. The natural palate of beer is quite savoury: yeast, malt, roast and cereal all have a natural umami bias which can really enhance a dish and give it more depth.

At the Michelin star level of beer- and food-matching, beer sommeliers look at each individual dish and find the perfect beer for it, and they pair them to enhance one another, each adding something special to the other. If you are providing neither Michelin star level food nor a beer sommelier all is not lost, there are some basic guidelines to follow to help you hit the high notes at home. As with all guidelines and generalisations there are two things to be aware of: the first is that your preferences and palate are unique and therefore you can't be wrong about what you like. The second is that whilst the following combinations and suggestions work in general, individual recipes and producers may vary to the point that the match no longer works. The key is to have fun and play around with these elements, finding your own matches and sweet spots.

### Contrast

Sometimes the coming-together of two distinct elements has a positive impact, the contrast creating a form of counterbalance and delicious tension. This should be done with beers and food with a similar flavour intensity, so neither side overwhelms the other.

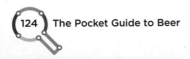

Hops are a great example of this; in contrast to fatty or oily food their bitterness creates a refreshing offset, often in conjunction with carbonation, leaving the palate fresh and quenched. So ales, pale ales and IPAs on the Aromatic Line and Explorer Loop tend to be a great match with everything from fish and chips to tempura vegetables. You can pair a pretty chunky IPA with the oiliness of fish and chips, but will need something with more restrained hops, like a British IPA or an American Pale Ale with the tempura.

In the main, if there is a flavour in the beer that reflects a condiment – like a chutney or pickle – then the beer will play that role in the dish. So a Fruit Lambic which is both fruity and sour will work like a chutney in cheese dishes or with cold meats.

## Complement

One of the obvious ways of pairing flavours is to look for similarities and let them meld together; this gives a seamless connection between beer and food. Be aware that sometimes this can result in a sense of sameness, so don't overdo it. As with when you are contrasting beer and food, you should balance the intensity of flavours so neither side dominates. One of the easiest ways to think about complementary flavours is to consider the roast on a beer and on the food: they will both have been through the Maillard reaction and have the resultant roasted, umami flavours. A great example is steak and something from the Central Line, particularly at the far left around the Dubbel and Doppelbock end. Also anything with grassy flavours like avocado and good olive oil will be enhanced by pairing it with a beer with the similarly grassy flavours found in American hops. Pair an IPA with your smashed avo on toast and you'll get an explosion of herbs, grass and green things.

## Spicy food

The first rule of spice is don't amplify it, which alcohol does, so steer clear of bruising alcohol levels if you've got a lot of chilli, ginger or black pepper in a dish. Hops also have a negative impact on spice so best to avoid them or make sure that your hoppy beer also has a good dose of sweeter malt in it. The sweetness in any beer will tone down the heat of a dish, which means the bottom end of the Aromatic Line is perfect with spicy dishes, especially Asian flavours. Both Weissbier and Witbier have a hint of sweetness, aren't too hoppy and they even have spicy coriander notes, all of which make them great partners to fragrant, spicy dinners. Because Witbier's recipe includes coriander, it makes a great match to fresh spicy dishes with coriander, for example Mexican salsas. You can also try a sweeter malted beer for the same reason.

## Cheese

Beer and cheese is a match made in heaven, and it's easy to experiment and play with the variables of complements and contrasts until you find your magic spots. Beer both refreshes the palate (see above notes) and complements dishes with similar flavours.

- ○ **Central Line beers** work well with nutty, aged cheeses like Gouda, Gruyère, mountain cheeses and some cheddars, as long as they aren't too mature.
- ○ **Aromatic Line beers** work with fresh, tangy cheeses like goat's cheese, feta and young cheddars, and big hop flavours also work well with a more developed cheddar.
- ○ **Creamy, farmyardy cheeses** need a balance of contrasting flavour, so the bottom right-hand corner of the BeerTubeMap provides some good options, either punchy IPAs or Saison on the Aromatic Line and Discovery Line or Lambics and Gueuze on the Epicurean Line.

- **Indulgence Line beers** complement big cheeses, especially blue ones.
- **Barley Wine** is by far the closest thing to a sweet or fortified wine on the BeerTubeMap and it lives up to its wine link when it comes to cheese. Try it with blue cheese, oozing camembert or mature cheddar. Its sweetness offsets the powerful flavours and the intense raisin character brings the fruit character of the cheese to the fore.

A great way to try this out is to gather a few friends, make up a varied cheeseboard, ask everyone to source beer from a different line on the map and then try all the combinations. Cheese and beer heaven!

### Sweet things

The key point with sweet things is to balance the sugar levels of the beer with the sugar levels of the dessert; if your beer isn't sweet enough it will taste bitter against your sweet thing. Which means most Pale Ales, IPAs and unsweetened stations on the Epicurean Line are out.

- Look to **wheat-based beers** for lighter desserts and cakes like pancakes, waffles and tarts.
- For **chocolate and heavier desserts** head to the Indulgence Line, where the chocolate and coffee flavours of Porter, Coffee Stout and Milk Stout play on those intense flavours.
- Head to the **Central Line** for a more nuanced approach, the stations between the Indulgence and Discovery Lines have enough sweetness to work with desserts but they also have a yeasty, umami element which works especially well with sweet pastry and baked desserts like crumble and bread and butter pudding.

## Smoky things

Smoke flavours and smoking are becoming increasingly popular in food and drink. More restaurants are smoking and charring on open flames and bartenders are incorporating whiffs of smokiness into high-end cocktails. Smoky beers can be surprisingly versatile when it comes to food pairing; they can be used either to complement dishes with charred ingredients, or the smoky flavour can be an interesting addition to a dish without any smoke, to add more depth.

- **O** **Smoky lagers, like Rauchbier,** are a great accompaniment where smoke is already used in a dish, such as smoked salmon, carbonara and other dishes with smoked bacon. The lager brewing method means it is light enough not to overpower the delicate flavours, but will add another smoky dimension. Lager also works with lighter smoked meats like pork ribs, as long as the overall flavour of the food isn't too punchy.
- **O** **Heavier smoked beers** that sit along the Indulgence Line are a great match for smoked meats and heavier marinades, especially if there's a bit of chilli in the mix.
- **O** **Sour beers** on the Epicurean Line will almost tone down the smoke in a dish, bringing out the other umami flavours that are linked with smoking and charring.

## HAVING FUN WITH BEER AT HOME

Not that many people need instruction in this! If you're intent on learning more about beer then there are some easy ways of exploring whilst hanging out and having fun. If you can combine not taking it seriously with taking it seriously then you're onto a winner.

1. **Always taste beers side by side**
   Having two glasses of beer is fun anyway. But always being in comparison mode makes it much easier to identify

differences and put words to them. Which in turn means you get to know what you do and don't like much quicker.

2. **Get a beer friend**

   Again, not hard. But if you've got someone else on the journey with you, it's easier to have the conversation about what flavour this or that is, without people looking at you like you've lost the plot. It's also a great excuse to see your mates more often and to share the costs of the beer buying!

3. **Invest in some good beer glasses**

   Amazingly, pint glasses stolen from your local pub during the last World Cup may not be the best vessel to showcase a beer. So instead, buy some good beer glasses, ideally tulip-shaped with a stem. The shape focuses the flavour and the stem means you don't warm the beer up as you hold it. Put them on your Christmas/Birthday list and you'll avoid stripey socks for ever more. Of course, many styles of beer have a specific, traditional glass shape, so you could keep extending your glass collection by accumulating them all. For example Weissbier is almost always served in the delicate, tall thin glasses, but if you don't have them, a tulip glass will work just as well.

4. **Hold your own beer crawls**

   To give your tasting sessions some shape pick a line on the BeerTubeMap and follow it all the way along, tasting each pair or three beers (depending on how many glasses you have) side by side. That way you can see the progressions in flavour as you taste and you'll have a clear start and end point. Each line is designed to be its own journey so you'll have a wide enough selection that there will be beers you like more and less as you go. If you've got a group of willing friends you can each bring a beer on the line or each host a different line. You won't drink any more than you normally would and will very quickly increase your beer skills. You could also do this in a craft bar if they serve small measures and have a wide enough range, although it will be more expensive.

## ADVANCED MANOEUVRES

### Go local

The great thing about beer at the moment is that it is impossible to keep up with all the new beers that breweries are producing. So once you've found the zones you like to hang out in on the BeerTubeMap, start exploring the nuances within that zone, use the recommendations on the map to try different versions of the same station and work out if you can hone your preferences. If you can you might be able to apply them to other stations. For example, you might really enjoy British IPAs made with the Citra hop, so find other beers that use that hop and see if you like them too.

### Go wide

The opposite of going local is going wide, push your boundaries to try the most extreme versions of the lines you like, and/or the beers that are furthest away from your preferences. Sometimes you will enjoy something with a completely different texture, flavour or taste more than something that is only a couple of stations away from your favourite.

### Eat!

Test the beer matching recommendations yourself.

○ Decide on a cuisine, Japanese, cheese, pizza, roast dinner, whatever floats your boat.

○ Bring in an assortment of dishes, either shop-made or takeaway, or push the boat out and make your own.

○ Buy a selection of beers from different lines. Pour them into glasses and label them so you know which is which.

○ Try everything with everything and see what works, and what doesn't. Keep your own notes and next time you're entertaining serve the best matches.

# Troubleshooting

Despite a brewer's best intentions, sometimes things don't end up going entirely to plan and beers are released with off flavours, or develop them after the packaging process. Although they are widely considered unpleasant, everybody has a different detection threshold for these flavours, and something that you can't bear to be near might happily be slurped up by your mate. Make sure you know when to legitimately take your pint back with this brief guide.

| The symptoms | The fault | The cause | The solution |
|---|---|---|---|
| **Rancid butter/ Popcorn/ Butterscotch aroma** People's threshold to this differs greatly so your mates may not notice it. | Diacetyl | Brewery has rushed conditioning. If the beer had been left longer, the diacetyl would have been naturally reprocessed by the yeast. | 😐 It won't hurt you, but don't drink it unless you really want to. If you're in a bar, take it back, but be diplomatic. |
| **Sweetcorn aroma** Also perceived as cold tomato soup and stewed green vegetables. | DMS (dimethyl sulfide) | A rushed production process when the beer has not been boiled for long enough. Or a result of bacterial infection. | 😐 It won't hurt you, but don't drink it unless you really want to. If you're in a bar, take it back, but be diplomatic. |

| The symptoms | The fault | The cause | The solution |
|---|---|---|---|
| Rotten eggs or struck match aromas. | Sulphur | Mass production. Yeast that is over-stressed and not fed enough. | ☺ Keep hold of it and see if it goes away – it should. If it doesn't, don't drink it unless you really want to. |
| Stale, musty, sherry notes, dark brown beer. | Over-oxidation | Beer is exposed to oxygen at some point of the process. | ☹ For some beers this is intentional, but if you weren't expecting the flavour it's probably wrong. Send it back. |
| Pear drops, foam banana or nail varnish remover. | Esters | Poor temperature control in fermentation. | ☹ For some beers this is intentional, but if you weren't expecting the flavour it's probably wrong. Send it back. |
| Musty, wet cardboard. | Trichloro-acetic acid (TCA – similar to cork taint in wine) | A specific form of mould. | ☹ Sadly, this will not get better or change. Send it back. |
| TCP or over-brewed tea flavours. | Overly phenolic beer | | ☹ Sadly, this will not get better or change. Send it back. |

| The symptoms | The fault | The cause | The solution |
|---|---|---|---|
| Murky or cloudy beer | Lack of filtration *or* Chill filtration | A brewery decides whether or not, and how much, to filter their beer. More filtering leads to clearer beer, but some flavour will be removed in the process. Brewer's choice. Chill haze happens when molecules in the beer bind at low temperature. | ☺ This depends somewhat on style, for example the Lager Line should all be crystal clear. Unless this is combined with any of the other issues it's a matter of taste. Let the beer warm up slightly and the haze will clear. |

# Glossary

**% ABV** % alcohol by volume. A unit of measurement for alcoholic strength.

**Acetobacter** A strain of bacteria that converts alcohol (ethanol) into acetic acid and spoils beer with a vinegar flavour.

**Acidulated malt** A variety of malt that can be used to control the pH level of a mash. After kilning the malt undergoes a lactic fermentation when the lactic acid produces bacteria that reside in the grain, resulting in a lactic acid content of approximately 1–2 per cent by weight.

**Adjunct** An ingredient used in brewing other than water, malted barley, hops or yeast.

**Ale** One of the two first branches of the beer family tree. Fermented warm with a top-fermenting yeast strain.

**Alpha acids** Acids found in hops that are isomerised in the boil to create bitterness in beer.

**Bag in box** A type of dispense method used largely by cider producers, but also occasionally by lambic producers. Basically a large plastic carton with a pouring valve on it, housed in a cardboard box to prevent the carton from being pierced.

**Bavaria** The largest state in Germany, and home to the world's best lager producers. The annual Oktoberfest festival takes place in the state's capital, Munich.

**Bottle conditioning** A packaging method for beer where a deliberate refermentation in the bottle results in natural carbonation.

**Bottom fermenting** Referring to yeast strains that operate at lower temperatures, causing them to grow more slowly and sink to the bottom due to having a smaller surface area. These yeasts are used for producing lager.

***Brettanomyces* (Brett)** A family of 'wild' yeasts typically seen as a spoiling agent in beer. However, some styles rely upon the flavours it produces and it is sometimes used intentionally. Can ferment some sugars that regular *Saccharomyces* can't. Although it produces low levels of acetic acid when oxygen is present, Brett is not typically considered a souring agent.

**Candi sugar** A type of sugar used in brewing, typically in Belgian styles. Will ferment right out, so contributes to ABV without leaving anything over to add body.

**Coolship** A wide and shallow tray, typically made from copper. Mostly used by lambic brewers to cool wort overnight, as the large surface area allows heat to dissipate into the atmosphere quickly. While the wort is exposed it becomes inoculated with wild yeast and bacteria. Derived from the original Flemish name (*koelschip*).

**Dextrins** The small parts of sugars that are left over by enzyme conversion in a mash. Too large for yeast to ferment into alcohol, so they remain in the finished beer to give body or residual sweetness.

**Dextrose** A 100 per cent fermentable sugar, occasionally used by brewers to help hit higher ABVs without contributing flavour or body.

**Diastatic power** This is the measure of how much starch-converting enzyme a malt contains.

**Enzyme** A biological catalyst that breaks down and metabolises complex molecules into smaller ones. In brewing we typically refer to alpha-amylase and beta-amylase, which break down long-chain sugars into smaller ones that the yeast can consume.

**Ester** The combination of an acid molecule and an alcohol molecule. In brewing these express themselves as various strong fruity aromas.

**Fermenter** The vessel in which yeast converts the sugars in wort to alcohol and carbon dioxide.

**Foeder** A large wooden vat for fermenting or ageing beer in. Typically used in the production of sour beers.

**Grist** The grain bill, or grain recipe, for the wort of a beer.

**Growler** A re-sealable, airtight vessel, usually made of glass or stainless steel.

**Husk** The thin outer coating of a seed. In brewing this typically refers to the husk on barley, which is useful for clarifying wort.

**IBU** International Bitterness Units, a measurement of bitterness in beer – however this cannot be a true measure of bitterness perception.

**Kettle** The vessel in a brewery used to boil wort.

***Lactobacillus*** A strain of bacteria that converts sugar to lactic acid. Used for making beers with a clean sour taste, but also used for production of yoghurt, pickles and other fermented foods.

**Lactose** An unfermentable sugar, comprised of a glucose molecule bonded to a galactose molecule. Also the sugar found in milk.

**Malt** Barley that has been allowed to begin germination. The main source of sugar for brewers.

**Mash** The mix of grains and water produced in a brewery.

**Oxidation** A process that occurs when beer comes into contact with free oxygen. Can be used to create complex sherry-like flavours, or can be a disastrous off flavour tasting like cardboard.

**Phenol** A highly aromatic and easily volatile organic acid. In beer terms these can be used to create a pleasantly spicy aroma.

**Protected appellation** A legally protected term that designates geographic origin.

***Reinheitsgebot*** The German Beer Purity Law of 1516 that stipulated that beer could only be made from barley, hops and water. The law does not refer to yeast explicitly, as its role in alcoholic fermentation was not yet established.

**Rye** A flavoursome grain used in baking and brewing to contribute an earthy, spicy flavour.

**Saccharomyces** The genus of fungus that 'brewer's yeast' (*Saccharomyces cerevisiae*) belongs to. The first part literally translates to sugar mould, while *cerevisiae* comes from the Latin for beer.

**Session beer/sessionable** A term used for a refreshing beer suitable to be drunk over the course of an evening. 'Session' isn't a formal term but it tends to refer to beers with a lower alcohol level and lighter palate.

**Sucrose** A sugar composed of a molecule of glucose bonded to a fructose molecule. Not directly fermentable, needs to be broken down by the enzyme invertase.

**Ticker** Somebody who likes to chase every new beer to 'tick it off' a list. Typically would use ratebeer.com or untappd.com.

**Trader** Somebody who uses beers from their collection to swap for others.

**Trappist** Trappist beers must be produced within the walls of one of the eleven Trappist monasteries in the world, and according to the practices and rules decided by the monks. The profit from the sale of these beers must be used solely for the upkeep of the abbey or social causes in the community.

# Beer index

Find your favourite beer in the list to identify which station best represents it. For example Beavertown Gamma Ray is an example of American Pale Ale.

Black Isle Hibernator → Oatmeal Stout 93
Boon Framboise → Fruit Lambic 112
Boon Gueuze → Gueuze 107
Boulevard Ginger Lemon Radler → Radler 29
Boulevard Tank 7 → Saison 49
Brains The Rev James → Old Ale 63
Brew By Numbers 03/ → Porter 94
Brew By Numbers 55/ → Double IPA 68
Brooklyn Brown Ale → Brown Ale 80
Brooklyn Lager → Vienna Lager 77
Brooklyn Local 1 → Belgian Golden Strong Ale 54
Brooklyn Summer Ale → Golden Ale 40
Bruery Terreux Oude Tart → Flanders Red 106
Brugse Zot Blond → Belgian Blond 47
Brugse Zot Tripel → Tripel 57
Budweiser Budvar → Pilsner 32
Burning Sky Saison Anniversaire → Saison 49
Burning Sky Saison La Provision → Saison 49
Buxton/Omnipollo Lemon Meringue Ice Cream Pale → Fruit Beer 42
Buxton/Omnipollo Yellow Belly → Imperial Stout 96
Buxton Axe Edge → American IPA 45
Buxton Dubbel → Dubbel 82
Buxton Extra Porter → Coffee Stout 100
Buxton Rednik → Irish Dry Stout 92
Buxton Trolltunga (Sour) → Fruit Beer 42
Cantillon Grand Cru Bruocsella → Lambic 110
Cantillon Gueuze → Gueuze 107
Cantillon Kriek → Fruit Lambic 112
Cascade Sang Royal → Flanders Red 106
Celis Wit → Witbier 50
Chimay Rouge → Dubbel 82
Chimay White Cap → Tripel 57
Chorlton Brewery (various) → Dry Hop Sour 70
Cloudwater → Double IPA 68
Cromarty AKA IPA → American IPA 45
Cromarty Hit the Lip → Golden Ale 40
Cromarty Man Overboard → Double IPA 68
Cromarty Whiteout → White IPA 46
Crooked Stave Hop Savant → Dry Hop Sour 70
Dark Star Hophead → Golden Ale 40
De Cam Bosbessen → Fruit Lambic 112
De Cam Oude Gueuze → Gueuze 107
De Cam Oude Lambiek → Lambic 110
De Dochter van de Korenaar Crime Passionel → White IPA 46
De La Senne Brussels Calling → Belgian Blond 47
Delirium Tremens → Belgian Golden Strong Ale 54
De Molen Bommen & Granaten → Barley Wine 88
De Ranke XX Bitter → Belgian Blond 47

La Trappe Dubbel → Dubbel 82
La Trappe Quadrupel → Quadrupel 85
Left Hand Milk Stout → Milk Stout 98
Left Hand Travelin' Light → Kölsch 27
Lervig Hop Drop sour → Dry Hop Sour 70
Lindemans Cuvée René → Gueuze 107
Lost Abbey Angel's Share → Barley Wine 88
Lost Abbey Lost and Found → Dubbel 82
Lost Abbey Red Poppy → Flanders Red 106
Löwenbräu Oktoberfestbier → Festbier 35
Mad Hatter Tzatziki Sour → Berliner Weisse 53
Magic Rock Cannonball → American IPA 45
Magic Rock Clown Juice → Witbier 50
Magic Rock Rapture → Red Ale 64
Maisel's Weisse → Weissbier 51
Marble Manchester Bitter → Bitter 78
Mikkeller Beer Geek Breakfast → Coffee Stout 100
Mikkeller Beer Geek Dessert Edition → Imperial Stout 96
Mikkeller Spontandryhop → Dry Hop Sour 70
Modern Times Blazing World → Amber Ale 65
Moor/Fuller's Relentless Optimism → Extra Special Bitter 61
Moor Fusion → Old Ale 63
Moor Nor' Hop → Golden Ale 40
Moor Old Freddy Walker → Old Ale 63
Moor Return of the Empire → British IPA 67
Moor Revival → Bitter 78
Moor So' Hop → Golden Ale 40
Moritz → Premium European Lager 31
Mythos → Premium European Lager 31
New Belgium Accumulation → White IPA 46
North Coast Old Rasputin → Imperial Stout 96
Northern Monk (various) → Double IPA 68
Northern Monk Faith → American Pale Ale 43
Oakham Citra → American Pale Ale 43
Oakham JHB → Golden Ale 40
Old Chimneys Good King Henry Special Reserve → Imperial Stout 96
Omnipollo Noa Pecan Mud → Milk Stout 98
Oskar Blues Old Chub → Scotch Ale 86
Paulaner Salvator → Doppelbock 84
Paulaner Wiesn → Festbier 35
Peroni Nastro Azzurro → Premium European Lager 31
Pilot Mochaccino → Coffee Stout 100
Pilot Mochaccino → Milk Stout 98
Pilsner Urquell → Pilsner 32
Piraat → Belgian Golden Strong Ale 54
Redchurch Great Eastern IPA → American IPA 45
Redchurch Urban Farmhouse Dry Hop Sour → Dry Hop Sour 70
Rochefort 10 → Quadrupel 85

# Acknowledgements

This project was a collaboration and collision of beer and wine worlds - thanks to Freya for being the catalyst.

**From Joe**
A heartfelt thank you to anyone who has ever talked beer, shared beer, or travelled in beer with me; every interaction has built towards this project. A specific thank you to my ever loving and patient partner Claudia, Mia (the cat), and my entire family. A huge thank you to Chris Mair and Calum Carmichael for giving me my first ever beer job, and to my good friends at James Clay and New Wave for putting up with what that has led to. For their help and specific advice on technical aspects, love to my friends Jonathan Hamilton, Sandy McKelvie, Colin Stronge, Dominic Driscoll and Johannes Weiss.

**From Nikki**
Adding beer to the Tube Map family has been a delicious adventure - thanks to everyone who has taken the time to explore it with me and been bored by my new geekiness. Especially Ged, for his unwavering support and annoying clarity when it's most needed. Thanks, too, to the growing Tube Map family, especially India, Blair and now Joe. And the maps wouldn't happen without Kirstie's patience and design skills - thanks for the final, final, final tweaks!

We had obviously had to try a lot of beer in the process. Chris at Cork and Cask helped out with the random beer selections and provided cheery chat . . . Thanks, pal!

# References

Once you've opened the door to beer you may find yourself wanting to learn more. Here are some sources that may help you on your beer adventure (though these are by no means definitive), listed alphabetically:

## Books

*Beer is for Everyone!*, Em Sauter (One Peace Books, 2017)
*Brew Britannia*, Jessica Boak and Ray Bailey (Aurum Press Ltd, 2017)
*Cooking with Beer*, Mark Dredge (Dog 'n' Bone, 2016)
*Farmhouse Ales*, Phil Markowski (Brewers Publications, 2004)
*Malt*, John Mallett (Brewers Publications, 2014)
*Mikkeller's Book of Beer*, Mikkel Borg Bjergso and Pernille Pang
  (Jacqui Small LLP, 2015)
*Radical Brewing*, Randy Mosher (Brewers Publications, 2004)
*The Oxford Companion to Beer* (ed.) Garret Oliver (OUP, 2011)
*The Little Book of Craft Beer*, Melissa Cole (Hardie Grant Books, 2017)

## Websites/apps

bjcp.org – the industry standard in beer classification
barclayperkins.blogspot.co.uk
belgiansmaak.com
beerhunter.com
boakandbailey.com
goodbeerhunting.com
draftmag.com
lambic.info
ratebeer.com
untappd.com

## People

Melissa Cole http://www.letmetellyouaboutbeer.co.uk @melissacole
Matthew Curtis @totalcurtis
Zak Avery http://thebeerboy.blogspot.co.uk @ZakAvery
Breandán Kearney @BreandanKearney
Will Hawkes @Will_Hawkes
Dina Slavensky @msswiggy
Lily Savage @QueerBeerBrewCo
Dominic Driscoll @ThornbridgeDom
Colin Stronge @ColinStronge